Fellow Nigerians, I Wish You Good Luck

Fellow Nigerians, I Wish You Good Luck

Reflections on Cleverness, Good Governance and Good Luck

Temitope O. Oyetomi

Baal Hamon Publishers

Akure   London   New York

ISBN-10: 9784956519
ISBN-13: 978-9784956512

International Correspondence:
Baal Hamon,
27 Old Gloucester Street,
London,
WC1N 3AX,
England.

www.baalhamonpublishers.com
publishers@baalhamon.com

Dedication

To Dr. Goodluck Ebele Jonathan, *GCFR* – President, Federal Republic of Nigeria – whose first name and the history of his many "lucky" attainments, and his decision to contest in the 2011 presidential elections, inspired me to write this book.

And to the many Nigerian citizens and residents who go to bed hungry most nights, and live in penury, while even the exotic dogs of their wealthy neighbours have more than enough to eat.

Acknowledgements

I have many "adopted" brothers and sisters: friends, really, but we are like family. I call them "*aburos*", or "sons" and "daughters". One of them would usually tell me, "*Bros, I hope your big mouth won't kill you one day*". Now, I'm being rather big-mouthed in this present book. And if that might kill me, I wouldn't want to put other people in danger. So, I would thank each of you without mentioning your real names. I would rather use your common nicknames.

First, and most importantly, I would thank "BJ", my closest *aburo*. I usually tell you, "*You are the best of them, my right-hand man . . . my brother, my friend, my hero*". Man, thanks for standing by me, especially when that nearly fatal road accident fractured my right arm and left me one-armed for over three months. You didn't let me feel handicapped. You're still the best.

Then, I should thank "Witty" my friend and editor, we would always haggle and argue, and reconcile again. I should also thank my consultant editor, "Zainab" for working with me on this and other manuscripts. "My designer friend with many BBFs", thank you for the cover design and the many other designs.

Friends, *egbons*, and *aburos*, over the years too numerous to list – "Danfo", "Deejay", "Saga", "Boiler", "Dr. Steve", "High Dee", "Alfa Zuga", "Ebube", "Chief of Igbadun", "Lasisi", "Popsy", "Deyinka Bobo", "Punch the Ocean", "9th Hour", "Deyinka Drama", "Ozone", "Kayham", "Jackie Chess", "Archer", "Oyinbo", "Yinka, my Kid Sister", "Daughter, Wonder", "Yemi Sweden", "Yemi Canada", "Daughter, my ex-lover", "Prince" (aka "my friend at Ijapo" – now in the US), "Philo", "Sweet Nose", "Samuel Doe", "Foa", "Agag", "A.Y. -

O. C. Food", 'Samwise", "Aroblack", "Douggie", "Ejayiwola", "Goddons" "Jalingo", "Osaz", "Habeeb SUB", "Trumpet", "Kings", "Yomco", "T. Damus", "A.Y. Effizy", "Boyon", "Man Key", "D. J. Ex-German", "Son - I wish you only the best" . . . and so many others. I thank you all. Thanks for your various contributions to my life. My encounters with each and all of you shaped my perspectives of life over the years. We fought. We argued. We parted. We reconciled. **Through you all, I learnt to love and to hate and to love again.** It's made me whom I am today. You know, life could be so much fun – like a drama script. *"O funny sha. O da bi script. Awon wo lo ko script yi gan? Awon Orun lo ko script. Awa kan de nse ti wa"*. Thank you for the various roles you have played according to the script of life.

My closest family members – "Mama", "Iba Paul", "Auntie", "Borda" and "Beehee" – you have often been my greatest helpers in life, you are my heroes. It was often a half-home, but we made it a good home. Your strength, dignity and laughter in the face of dangers and sorrows are unique. You are my heroes. I can't say that too often. Invariably, your lives have been candles brought through the storms. It's a miracle that we are all still alive today, in spite of all the storms.

My full family, "Baba", "Iye Segun", "Iye Folake", and my brothers and sisters, it's quite painful to have grown up as one "separated from his brethren", but in spite of the polygamy – we are one family. I appreciate you all. "Auntie London", especially, and your family, you made my stays in London convenient.

Cousins. "MJ", with your sister and mum, thank you especially. I miss your dad every day. God understands. He was a very good man. Somehow, I picked from him the exclamation "Oh Father", as he would always say when he was tired. Thanks for my stays with you in London too.

The churches. The Pastors. The Chaplains. "Venerable Prof." and his family. The Chapel. "Pastor Prof. T. A." and family, "Pastor Prof Z. D." and family I appreciate you all.

"Baba" – as someone once sang, *"Baba l'oun se ohun gbogbo"*. I must appreciate you for your character. You are always true to yourself. Thank you, sir, for that "token". It was supportive indeed, but more important was the act in itself. Even though many ill lucks of our nation often becloud the sights of men from your enigmatic magnanimity, my encounters with you show me that sometimes men achieve true greatness at the expense of their own reputation.

To colleagues, bosses and students at the university where I have worked for these fifteen years – what more can I say? I practically grew up here and assumed that the whole campus was my laboratory for me to observe humans as specimens – through you all; **I have seen both the *divine* and *animal* natures of men.** On this campus, I have learnt to give and to take; to quarrel and to reconcile; to be bitter and to be joyful; **to offend and to forgive.** Above all, I have learnt both **to follow and to lead and to be self-reliant.** What a great opportunity! Thank you, all.

And you; thank you for getting a copy of this book. I hope it makes some sense to you by the time you have finished reading it.

CONTENTS

PREFACE

Dem no get craze. Abeg no be me talk am o. You would really need an aptitude for languages in order to catch up with me in this book, because I will insert here and there some sentences in the Nigerian Pidgin English and Yoruba. However, I will put a glossary on the book's complimentary website **www.goodluckbook.com** to help you decipher the italicised words.

The late Fela Anikulapo Kuti sang about democracy and interpreted it as "*demo*nstration of *craz*iness". Now, be careful, craziness is not always a bad thing. My American friends use the word very loosely that you often get confused whether craziness is good, or bad, or neutral. When the weather is harsh, and they don't like it, they will say "*it's crazy*". When they watch soccer – yeah, it's often "*soccer*", not football – and it thrills them, they will say "*the game is crazy*". So, whether they like it or hate it, it's always "*crazy*". Bestseller gospel artiste, Kirk Franklin, in one of his tracks said something like "*make some Holy Ghost crazy noise*"[1] to God! I would presume that he meant, "*get really positively excited about God and shout his praise*" or, whatever.

That's America. Here in Nigeria, there's no good interpretation of "crazy". Here, it's only when you want to start a fight that you can tell a man, "*you dey craze!*" So, Fela was actually *yabbing* "them" when he called it *democrazy*. I will not trail his path to *yab* anyone. I dare not. But I will use the word "crazy" like my American friends.

Nigeria is a crazy country and many Nigerians utterly demonstrate the craziness. You tell them *dem dey craze* and they'd be cross with you, *dem no go wan craze*. Or, rather you tell them *dem no get craze* and they'd be angry as well, *dem go wan*

---

[1] From the song *Hossana Forever* in album *The Rebirth of Kirk Franklin*

craze. So, whether you tell them they are crazy or not crazy, you will get a crazy response in as much as you use the "craze" word. If you describe them as crazy, they will crazily prove to you that they are not crazy.

Here people get really crazy about just anything you can think of – can you imagine this: a newspaper in Europe published a cartoon portraying the revered prophet of Islam as a terrorist, and the cars and buildings of people who knew nothing at all about the cartoon got damaged and burnt in Nigeria. I mean, people who did not even hear about the cartoon, or see it; and who, if they had heard about it would probably condemn the cartoon in the strongest terms, got attacked in Nigeria. That's crazy.

Statistics indicate that our economy has a GDP of $2500 per capita[2]. That's averagely more than $5 per head per day even in the leap years. Yet there are thousands of families that live on less than $1 per day. I mean $1 per family per day – while the international conventions recognise living on less than $1 per head per day as poverty. So, we are a country where there is sufficiency or even relative wealth, but it is not fairly spread. That's crazy.

Recently, I asked a 20-year-old undergraduate university student, *"How I can become a multimillionaire in the coming year?"*. He answered, *"You will either have to rob the bank or use a human being to make a ritual for money"*. Awwww! That's coming from a university student in the 21st-century. I mean, I had to lecture him that Mark Zuckerberg, founder of Facebook, is just a few years older than him and founded Facebook whilst he was yet a university undergraduate like him and is a billionaire today[3]. Of course, this young man was just joking – he wouldn't really mean I should go and rob the bank or use a human to make blood rituals for money. But the fact that he was bereft of any pragmatic and creative ideas, which is typical of the average Nigerian youth, is just sad. It's crazy. It's even crazier that most Nigerians still believe in money charms and everyone prays never to fall a victim to money-making rituals. (Don't you ever watch Nigerian home videos and movies? Don't you see how much of voodoo is

---

[2] The World Fact Book – Central Intelligence Agency
[3] http://en.wikipedia.org/wiki/Mark_Zuckerberg

often packed into the movies? Those movies act out the beliefs of most Nigerians).

I mean it's just crazy that a person would kill another human being and would believe that blood or body parts extracted from such would be used to make charms that would bring him or her vast wealth. I don't know how real it is; I have never witnessed such, and I don't wish to witness it. But most people here believe that it is a real practice. It's crazy.

The list of what could be crazy in Nigeria is inexhaustible. I could go on and on. The two craziest stuff here, though, are politics and religion. But I must quickly revert to where I started from – *democrazy*, the demonstration of craziness.

Nigeria is said to have returned to democracy in 1999 (as though indeed we ever truly had any democracy in the first place). We now have a legal public holiday called "Democracy Day". It's good. It's colourful. But it's also crazy. It marks the day civilians are normally sworn in as presidents and governors in our country after the last military rule. Yet the process through which the presidents and governors emerge is nothing less than crazy.

How do we explain a situation in which the gubernatorial elections in five contiguous states would be nullified one after another for reason of electoral malpractices? Look at it: Delta State shares borders with Edo State; Edo State shares borders with Ondo State; Ondo State share borders with Ekiti State; and Ekiti State shares borders with Osun State. As at Christmas 2010, where were all the governors that were sworn in on Democracy Day in 2007 in these states? The tribunals nullified their elections. It's crazy.

Yet there were elections and people voted. Votes were counted, although other stuff reportedly happened in the processes. In one of the tribunal hearings, a man appeared in court with one of his legs reportedly cut off during the violence that accompanied the elections. I saw in the Punch newspaper photographs of pressmen reportedly being assaulted and beaten while covering the elections. *Pressmen?* Yes. *That's crazy*. Of course.

In one state, the Resident Electoral Commissioner resigned, citing that her conscience did not agree with the results returned in the elections from some voting areas. Then we were told that her resignation did not succeed. She then returned to announce those same results. It's all democracy. *Abi o. Na so now.*

Let me confess, I have never voted in any election. I never believed in the process. I never had a voter's registration card. During the last elections in 2007, I was in a friend's house at Ijapo Estate in Akure. Usually, that area of Akure, the Ondo State capital, often had more regular power supply than the rest of the city. I knew I would be indoors throughout watching foreign action movies. That was more interesting to me than the elections. My friend was not voting too, although there was a polling station very close by. I was indoors enjoying a movie when he rushed into the room to call me; *"hey, 'Tope, come and see what's happening outside . . . they said the Deputy Governor is hijacking ballot boxes"*. I told him, *"None of my business, please. I didn't cast any vote and I could care less whatever happens to the votes that were cast"*. He was puzzled. *"Don't you think we should just go and see? . . . let's see if it's true, let's see if it's really the Deputy Governor"*. I told him, *"You go and see, I don't care; I don't want to see"*. Well, he was too chicken-hearted to go and confirm (I was chicken-hearted too, though) because things like that might go bloody. The next day, that story was in the papers. I cannot tell whether or not it was the truth, I just could care less. That's some crazy news and really crazy allegations but I doubt if that was successfully proven at the tribunals. I wasn't following the progress of the legal battle. I didn't care.

You know what? It's even funny to me that I am writing all these now and it's funnier that I managed to both register as a voter and plan to vote in the 2011 elections. Why? Have I finally found some courage to step out of my house during elections? Why am I even bold enough to decide to write a book about elections and governance in Nigeria? The reason is simple – I am doing these for good luck. I mean, really simple "good luck" and nothing more. It's crazy, isn't it?

See, elections in Nigeria are often crazy. You encounter a lot of crazy stuffs; posters on walls here and there. *Paper posters for elections in the 21st century?* Of course. (Apparently, we are still in the previous century and we need a lot of catching up to do). But then, you also hear a lot of promises on radio and TV. Promises of good roads, potable water, regular power supply, free education, free health, free this, free that, . . . as though we have not always been hearing that. *Na today?*

Really, I don't mind all that but when it comes to people allegedly losing their legs over votes, that's the really scary part . . . and it scares the . . . (you know what) out of me! But lately, there have been these chit-chats about luck – goodluckism – in the newspapers and online and it comes to a point where I can't really stomach my comments any more about all of it. I would like to say a few things – I have always had the stomach to say them but not the guts and if I have some good luck too, I won't lose my jugular and gut after saying a few things in this book. The way I see it, there is always interplay between good governance, cleverness and good luck. That's all I want to say, my style of saying it – as well as the details I dig up in saying it – may be poignant, pungent or pleasant . . . or all of the above. It's all crazy, you know. But wherever this offends, please forgive me. I don't intend to offend anyone.

There's this stuff my friend at Ijapo once told me. I didn't witness it, so, it may not have been true. But it could just as well have been true. *Dis na Naija and anything fit happen.* You know, he said there was a gentleman who was easing himself by the roadside. It's not unusual here for people to stop by the roadside and urinate into the bush, or street drainage, or fence, or even the corner walls of a building. This young man was doing the usual when he noticed the rather unusual – a lunatic man was walking towards him, brandishing a cutlass. The young man had to cut his flow and take to his heels. But no sooner had he began to run than the lunatic man also started running after him, chasing him hotly. The young man ran into a petrol station at the gate of Ijapo Estate for refuge. The pump attendants there simply yelled on the lunatic man *"common, go back . . . go back!"* and the lunatic man quietly turned back without hurting anyone. *Sounds far-fetched. Tell it to nursery school children.* But you never can tell. It could have been true. I believed him anyway. You've got to see the excitement in his eyes as he was sharing the gist; *"una see wetin I see today?"* – he blurted out. You know, I was saying that if the young man had not run, it was possible the lunatic may just have passed him by without attacking him. It was just a possibility but the guy left nothing to chance. If that story was true, that's some real luck! Because when you deal with crazy people and crazy situations, you never can tell how exactly things will go. You will ultimately need good luck to pull through.

Now, electioneering has begun. It's time again for *democrazy* – a time when, if history repeats itself, craziness will be blatantly demonstrated. Sincerely, I wish and I pray that what we would get from the 2011 elections will be truly democracy and not democrazy. Yet the best I could do, friends, is to write this crazy little book and also wish you good luck as you go out to support your favourite candidates and cast your votes . . . I also wish our nation as a whole a very good luck, especially in the presidential elections which already has a lot of testy issues involved. In fact, I wish you only the best. Please kindly wish my big mouth, and life and limb, some good luck too.

I started writing this book in the last quarter of 2010. Somehow, I have had to keep writing and rewriting everyday because each morning the newspapers bring some scenic additions to the drama already playing out. I just have to stop now and go to press or else, I will never finish the book and you will never read it. If you really care to follow through, join me online at www.goodluckbook.com and let the discourse continue from there.

Blessings.

Temitope
Akure, March 2011.

PART I

2011 Elections and Beyond

Chapter 1

I Stand Where God Stands

"2011: I Stand Where God Stands – Obasanjo"
- The Punch Newspaper, Sunday, 3 October, 2010.

OBJ Stands Where God Stands

The Nigerian nation seems perennially enchanted with former president, Olusegun Obasanjo. Even when he merely sneezes or claps, it makes headlines. And people would like to seek interpretations and meanings to it. I'm not surprised. He has ruled Nigeria longer than any other person – he spent 3 years as a military head of state from 1976 to 1979 and then 8 years as civilian President, from 1999 to 2007. Men who were toddlers during his military rule were already fathers during his comeback. And the fathers? They already became grandfathers. Thus, it would seem the attention of the nation never left him.

You see, OBJ – as he is popularly called – has done quite a lot for this country. He is one of the very few people who believe that the unity of the country is sacrosanct and has always contrived to see that the country does not fall apart. But Nigeria is a very complex country; leaders and followers are permanently polarised. There are endemic problems in Nigeria that are so grotesque and at once ghostly, such that you recognise that problems exist but find it hard to define *who* the problems are. (I used the personal pronoun "*who*" because the problems seem to be living entities – growing bigger and stronger, copulating with other problems, giving birth to newer problems, and eventually dying off and leaving behind more problems as survivors).

One of the basic problems we have in this country is that the leaders don't trust the followers and the followers don't trust the leaders. Everyone tries to blame the problems on someone else. And wherever you go, you will always hear

1

people talking about "*dem*" – the nameless "them" – "*dem talk say*" . . . "*dem don do*" . . . "*dem don carry*" . . . only God knows "*who dem be*".

And that brings me to the point . . . "*only God knows*" . . . Seriously speaking, one would think Nigeria is the most God-loving country on earth. Hardly would Nigerians not talk about God in anything they do. Even atheists and pagans in Nigeria talk about God and so do millions of Christians and Muslims, the two largest religious groups in Nigeria, even while fighting one another, burning places of worship and butchering fellow humans.

October 3, 2010. The papers were awash with OBJ's comments about standing where God stands in regard to the 2011 elections. Some reporters had managed to catch up with him at the airport. (It looks like reporters are always waylaying OBJ at airports; they will always tell us that they asked him questions at the presidential lounge of this airport or that airport. There was even the news of OBJ being attacked by a "madman" at one airport . . . beating airport security and OBJ's security aides to force his way into OBJ's car.[4]

> There are endemic problems in Nigeria that are so grotesque and at once ghostly, such that you recognise that problems exist but find it hard to define who the problems are.

Reporters said they had asked OBJ where he stands on the 2011 elections and he had answered "*I stand where God stands*". They further asked him, "*Where does God stand?*". He told them, "*You go and ask God*".

See, as a preacher, I have the prerogative to tell you where God stands, if OBJ declined. I wouldn't say he didn't know where God stands, because for him to have said he stands where God stands, he must have already assumed that there is a particular position that God assumes. However, talking

---

[4] The Punch – 9th November 2010

to the average Nigerian is often complex. You see, Nigerians will interpret whatever you say to them according to the meanings found in their local languages and understanding such that when they report it, the meaning would have metamorphosed from what you originally meant. I can bet that there will be wide and wild interpretations of what I will be saying in this book.

The other day, OBJ reportedly said that even if Jesus Christ himself had conducted elections in Nigeria, Nigerians would still say that the election was not free and fair. The matter however generated so much fuss. Churches sermonised about it. Some even made press conferences. Some said he blasphemed. I still don't see the blasphemy in this. The import of the comments as I see it is that Nigerians cannot be fully pleased. He was not saying that Jesus Christ is incompetent but rather that Nigerians are insatiable. That's normal; humans generally are insatiable.

Do you read the Bible? Even in the Bible, when Jesus performed healing, some people disputed the genuineness of his miracles and authority. How much more do you think people would accept it, if Jesus were to be the Chairman of INEC (Independent National Electoral Commission – the body responsible for the conduct of governmental elections in Nigeria)?

Nigerians are often sentimental about religion and ethnicity. I mean, crazily sentimental.

See, Nigerians are often sentimental about religion and ethnicity. I mean, crazily sentimental. The country has a predominantly Christian south and a predominantly Moslem north. Most likely, if Jesus Christ were a Nigerian, he would be a southerner. (That's going by the logic that most people in the country simply follow the religion of their parents or that prevalent religion of their ancestral community without having their own real and original choice in the matter. Thus, most people born in northern Nigeria would be Moslems, and most born in the southern Nigeria would be Christians – just blindly following the religions without personally seeking to understand what life is all about).

3

Now, if Jesus were INEC Chairman, and managed to conduct an election that was very free and fair – possibly perfect – and it happened that a southerner or Christian won the election; the next day, you would hear some people beginning to accuse Jesus of electoral fraud. They would say, "Jesus rigged the elections in favour of tribesman and follower". So, then, that's the point, the average Nigerian just wants someone from his family or town or state or religion to win the elections. It rarely matters whether such a person is competent or not. Indeed and in truth, that is not where God stands.

God Will Give Us Good Leaders

Let me dare to tell you this. I used to attend a prayer meeting programme in the early 1990s. A group of churches pulled together and we often prayed for a better Nigeria. You know what? At the prayer meeting, we were majorly southerners. There was a prominent presidential aspirant from the South – M. K. O. Abiola – he was a Moslem. At our prayer meetings, we would often pray against Abiola's success in the election. The prayer leaders would tell us that *"Abiola is a Moslem; he has plans to Islamise the country. Pray that God will stop him from becoming president"*. And the congregation would pray fervently. I knew I would not be voting, but I joined the prayers and often prayed as directed.

It turned out that there was a presidential election on June 12, 1993. Abiola is popularly believed to have won that election. But the election was annulled by the then military regime. I had to wonder if that was an answer to the prayers we made at those prayer sessions. I would leave that to debate.

I believe in prayers. I believe in divine interventions. I believe that God answers prayers. But what I see here is that Nigerians believe more in prayers than they actually believe in God. Someone might read this account of the prayers we made against M.K. O. Abiola and begin to hate us for it. Indeed, if it was our prayers that stopped Abiola from becoming president, which I would rather believe was not, our own responsibility in the matter was just saying the prayers, but the Person that answered our prayers carries the ultimate responsibility. I mean, if it was really our prayers that stopped Abiola.

God knows I can never be a part of such prayers today. Why? Because I know better now. It no longer matters to me whether whoever becomes president in

4

this country is a Moslem or a Christian. It doesn't matter whether he is from the North or the South. I don't care if it's only the Hausas that become presidents for the next 200 years non-stop, or whether it is the Igbos. God doesn't stand in the midst of confusion and divisions and separations and tribalism. God stands in the midst of unity, where the people are of one mind and one accord. God stands where the people desire true justice and fairness.

I like the Bible. It's more a collection of books than it is actually a single book. According to the Bible, David – Israel's most famous king – wrote about where God stands in regard to governmental authority. His words: *"He who rules over men must be just, ruling in the fear of God"*. (2 Samuel 23: 3). That's where God stands.

He who rules over men must be just. It doesn't matter whether "he who rules over Nigeria" is a northerner or a southerner or whether he or she is a Christian or Moslem. So far as the person is just and fair, and progressively minded, that is all that matters.

I'm sick and tired of this *na-my-broda-dey-there* attitude. Since all these days when *na una broda dey there*, what has it benefited the nation? See, Nigerians must move beyond the sentiments that the presidency must go the north or come to the south or move east or west. Every time, I hear stuff like *"let's rotate the presidency"*, it only reminds me of nursery and primary school pupils playing with toys. I mean, the presidency is not just some teddy bear or Plasticine – *"give me, it's my turn to play with it, you have played with it for 4 years now"*. Is the seat of the president meant to be some child's rocking chair? Common, that's how it always sounds whenever you bring up this "let's-rotate-it" debate; it's sickening. I mean,

It no longer matters to me whether whoever becomes president in this country is a Moslem or a Christian. It doesn't matter whether he is from the North or the South.

elsewhere people seek to become presidents on the basis of how pragmatic they are, not on the basis of where they come from.

The Americans are lucky. I would say they stand where God stands. If not, Barack Obama would not have been President. You know, his father was Kenyan, his mother American. He was born in America. This qualified him to contest for the office of the president of the United States. The truth is that if Obama's mother were Nigerian, and his father Kenyan, and he was born in Nigeria, he would never be president in Nigeria. Even if he is legally qualified, people won't vote for him. They would say he is Kenyan and not Nigerian.

. . . the presidency is not just some teddy bear or Plasticine – "give me, it's my turn to play with it, you have played with it for 4 years now".

I have friends of Igbo descent who were born here in Akure. They grew up here. They have been here all their lives. Yet they are always regarded as "foreigners". I mean, in their own country – on the very soil they were born! When shall we grow up as a nation? When shall we mature? When shall we become Nigerians and stop being Igbos, Hausas, Ijaws, Yorubas *et cetera*? When shall we become – according to the words of our national anthem – "one *nation bound in freedom, peace and UNITY*"?

To become a nation truly BOUND in FREEDOM, PEACE and UNITY, is where God stands. And as our nation prepares to vote in the 2011 elections, and in fact, in subsequent elections, I urge us to stand where God stands. Let's put aside tribal, ethnic and religious sentiments and cast our votes justly for the brilliant minds, the just persons and the God-fearing individuals.

See, I have often abstained from voting because I always wondered if the men we vote for really have true hearts for the nation. However, this year, I decided I would vote and urge people to vote and encourage people to be more involved in government. If it is called democracy, we shouldn't continue to make it

6

democrazy – we should endeavour to make it *"a government of the people by the people for the people"*[5] (as was suggested to the American people by Abraham Lincoln in his famed Gettysburg Address). We should engage the government the more, and trim down the powers of the rulers by enthroning the law above them. The weakness of the law has been the bane of our country. Men go into government to live above the law. It shouldn't be like that forever; there should be a change. But change wouldn't come if we don't make the change. Did I hear you say, *"God will bring a change to our country"*? Of course, I knew you will say that. *Na God dey do everything for Naija.*

God Will Pack Our Faeces

In Nigeria, we have been for too long a people that expect God to do everything for us. *"God will give us good leaders"*. *"God will help our governments to build good roads"*. *"God will intervene in the health sector so our doctors won't go on strike again"*. In fact, if we have our way, Nigerians will also add, *"we don poo-poo, God go pack our poo-poo and help us clean our bum-bum"*. Like kids.

No. God is not like that. Once you attain the age of reasoning, and consent, you should be able to get most things done for yourself. In fact, the Bible says, *"The heaven, even the heavens, are the Lord's; But the earth He has given to the children of men"*. (Psalm 115: 16) I think that as individuals, yes, a good proportion of Nigerians are at least 18 years old and could be assumed to have reached the age of reasoning but as a country, the soul of the Nigerian nation is rather childish and immature.

So, would God give us good leaders in the next election? Nope, unless we elect good leaders by ourselves. Would God build good roads for us? Nope, that's our duty. Would God stop our doctors from going on strike?

> *The weakness of the law has been the bane of our country. Men go into government to live above the law. It shouldn't be like that forever;*

---

[5] http://en.wikipedia.org/wiki/Gettysburg_Address

God dey go hospital? Na we get hospitals, na we go do wetin go make our hospitals work well.

Most of these things we pray for in Nigeria and ask God to do for us are not God's duty, they are ours and it all begins with choosing right and voting right. That's why I will be voting this year and also putting my mouth where my vote goes.

In my growing up years, my elder brother – "Borda" – usually said to me that *"God never loses an election because God will wait for everyone to cast the votes, and whoever most people have voted for is whom God will cast his vote for"*. I will not go into the theological correctness or incorrectness of that. But it was Borda's way of interpreting *vox populi vox Dei*.

> If we have our way, Nigerians will also add, "we don poo-poo, God go pack our poo-poo and help us clean our bum-bum".

However, for *vox populi* to be truly *vox Dei*, we must first look for men who are just and God-fearing and elect such people. I mean, leaders with a caring heart.

I used to think that my personal vote was immaterial to the outcome of the elections. It's wrong thinking. If every vote is genuinely counted, then every vote will count. There was once an election for the post of the dean of a faculty in one university. The Board of Studies of that faculty comprised of 52 voting members. At the end of the day, the winner emerged with a 26-vote majority. A particular voting member was absent from the election, which made the votes go 26 against 25. A single vote made the difference. And your own single vote counts. That's where God stands.

Unnecessary and Expensive Voters' Registrations
See, the electoral system in Nigeria is at once funny and faulty. Billions of Naira are spent unnecessarily from time to time for the compilation of the voters' register.

Let me introduce some contention here. The voters' registration exercise closed in February; elections will hold in April. Normally people 18 years old and above are constitutionally eligible to vote. Many people will turn 18 in March. Even some people will turn 18 on the day before the election. Technically, they would not be eligible to vote just because they were not yet 18 in February. Is that constitutional? Elsewhere, such people would sue the government for violation of their constitutional rights unless provisions were made to register those who were expected to reach the voting age at the time of the elections. We need to change the way elections are done in Nigeria. But we would not be able to make that change if in the first place we don't elect people who are change-driven into offices. That is where God stands.

Ideally, there should be no need for a voters' register. People should just be able to use any government-issued photo ID that shows their date of birth to be accredited for voting. In advanced democracies, voters' register, (or "electoral roll"), are still being used, though. But there are sufficient checks and balances to ensure that people on the electoral rolls are as old as they claim to be. Possibly, we should require that for subsequent elections in Nigeria, government-issued photo Ids should be required for voters' registration.

A possible problem with this idea is that getting a government-issued photo ID in Nigeria is a problem in itself. Most people I know paid 16,000 Naira to get their international passports. No receipts are issued to them for the payment. That is not the official price but that is the going price. I was recently at a Police station and a police officer who saw me with me my passport asked how much I got it. I told him. Then, I was watching to see if he would react and protest the price. No, it didn't matter to him. *"I did mine for N18,000"* – he told me. He explained to me that he got it the same day, though. I understand. He understood. If you are Nigerian, you would understand. But the time has come when we should stop showing

But the time has come when we should stop showing understanding and sympathy to gross illegality.

9

understanding and sympathy to gross illegality.

The other day, I was at the Local Government Secretariat. I wanted to collect my National Identity Card, which I duly enrolled for at the appropriate time 2 years earlier. I hadn't bothered to go and collect it because I didn't really need it. I always had my international passport and driver's licence as photo IDs. One day, however, I decided to go and collect the National ID card. The officer checked the records and told me mine was not processed. There had been an error with the photograph and the ID was therefore not produced. "Okay", I asked her, "*can I register for a new one now?*". She answered, "*Yes, of course, why not? But you will have to come back when NEPA brings the light*". I understood. It's often called "*light*" and not "*electricity*". NEPA is the former name for the Power Holding Corporation of Nigeria, the company responsible for generating and distributing electric power supply in the country.

I asked the officer, "*How soon would it be possible for me to have the national ID card after registering at this time?*". She answered "*I don't know o, the ones we re-registered 2 years ago are yet to arrive.*" I laughed (the laughter was not in pleasure but scorn and derision). "*So, you mean if I register for a National ID card now, I may not have it for the next 2 years?*" – I asked her. "*Well, I cannot really say*", she responded. I told her, "*I see. Thank you, ma*".

All that has got to change. Corruption and inefficiency in the process of acquiring international passports, driver's licences, and national ID cards must stop. Instead of spending N84 Billion every 4 years to prepare and update voters' register, we can actually spend less than half of that to create a system that will purify the process of acquiring government-issued photo IDs and just require any of these for the elections. That's too late for this year's election. However, as we vote this April, we must carefully select leaders that have a vision to sanitise and purify the system.

My opinion is that the idea of registering people just for the sake of elections encourages a lot of fraud. Didn't you read the papers? Some newspapers reported that some politicians were buying off voters' registration cards as soon as the people registered. That's crazy. If it were your international passport, or national ID card, or driver's licence, you wouldn't sell it to any politician.

Besides, to register with INEC, no proof of your age is required. You only need to tell them any date of birth you like. You could be 72 and tell them you are 55. *Dem no send you.* But just as well, you could be 16 and claim that you are 18. How does INEC verify the age of voters? You tell me. However, getting a government-issued photo ID, such as a passport, would require evidence of date of birth. Our country should therefore stop wasting billions of Naira every now and then on voters' registration and voters' card. We don't really need it. We should rather seek to facilitate the ease of getting government issued photo IDs and see how these could be used for voters accreditation instead of a specifically designed voters registration card.

One of the reasons this has never been put underway is because our country generally lacks a planning attitude. We seem to dote and sleep until the events are already upon us and at once we are like a bunch of hungry kids. We can't ever wait for a systematic way of doing things that will endure to be created; all we want are quick-fixes.

If I should suggest here that whoever becomes President in 2011 should immediately initiate plans on the possible use of government-issued photo IDs in the 2015 elections, the response from most people would be *"why should we begin to talk about 2015 elections when the people we elect in 2011 have not started to do anything? That's not the priority. Electricity is priority. Good roads are priority. Education is priority."* The truth is that setting up a national committee to immediately begin work on using government-issued photo IDs, such as the national ID card, for 2015 does not prevent the government from fixing all these "priorities". If that aspect is not addressed as early as possible, the country will spend yet another 120 Billion Naira on voters' registration again in another 4 years. We have to create systems and stop using fire-

. . . we are like a bunch of hungry kids. We can't ever wait for a systematic way of doing things that will endure to be created; all we want are quick-fixes.

brigade approaches. It's not only about the leaders; it's also about the followers.

God Stands Where We Stand

I will be unfair to the truth if I don't state the reversal of the axiom, which is equally true. While it is good to stand where God stands, we must also recognise that God will often stand where we stand. God is the constant. We are the variables.

I like the philosophy of the other major religion. They would always be consoled that "*it is an act of God*", whenever they have seemingly tried their best and things yet go the other way. However, it will require extra-ordinary miracles for us all to vote *en masse* for a particular person and God will say "*no way, I reject your choice*". In most cases, God will let us do as we please – because "*the earth He has given to the children of men*"

> We cannot vote a thief into the office of the president of the country or governor of a state, and then turn around to pray that God should not let that thief steal our resources.

We cannot vote a thief into the office of the president of the country or governor of a state, and then turn around to pray that God should not let that thief steal our resources. Why else do you think he wanted to be president? Why else do you think he wanted to be the governor? Of course, just to steal, to kill and to destroy. Devils. We would have to mature as a nation and elect leaders on the basis of their characters and their logically provable plans to move the nation forward. Only when we make the right choices, can God help our nation. We can't continue to defecate in sacred places – on the altars of God and on the law – and expect God to pack our faeces.

I Will Consult God

Beware when wolves come to you in sheep's clothing. We have seen it too often. Leaders will come out to say that they have prayed and consulted God and God has asked them to run for a particular office. For instance, in the 2003 elections, a popular pastor joined the race for the office of the president. It was reported that he claimed that God told him he would be president of the country.

Personally, I believe that religious leaders should be politically neutral, especially in public. And so should the traditional rulers – royal heads of our cities, towns and villages – as well as pressmen. These people need to realise that they occupy positions of public trust and as such should maintain political neutrality in public as long as the public is heterogeneous.

We certainly need men who still listen to their consciences to lead this country.

Let me give you an example. The Queen of England has been the Head of State in her country since 1952 but there have been various governments from different political parties. Invariably, it is always "Her Majesty's Government". That's royalty. When the country is governed by the Labour Party, it's Her Majesty's Government; when the government is the Conservative Party, it is Her Majesty's Government; when the government is a coalition of the Conservative Party and the Liberal Democrats, it is still her Majesty's Government.

Here in Nigeria, it's different. Our majesties and highnesses run after politicians and publicly endorse some candidates. That's not regal enough. Remember, "*he that rules over men must be just*". True justice would begin to thrive in our country when royal fathers refrain from publicly endorsing politicians. The same is true of religious leaders.

Pastors and Imams must completely abstain from publicly endorsing politicians and political parties. As I prepare this book for press now, a very senior and popular pastor in Nigeria has accepted to run for the office of the vice-president of the country. Hmmn, what can I say? He's probably been a Christian before I was born, and I should not be the one teaching him what the Bible says. He would certainly have his own reasons for accepting to run for that post. I

13

appreciate the fact that he has a reputation of always speaking frankly about issues. When he was questioned, he answered that he never said that God had asked him to run for the office of the vice-president of the country. He said, and I will quote a particular newspaper, "*I am following my conscience*". That's good and exemplary. We certainly need men who still listen to their consciences to lead this country. Most other pastors would have said they have consulted God and that God gave them the go-ahead, others would have said, they were just doing their own things and God specifically called out to them and instructed them to run for the presidency or vice-presidency.

> We can't continue to defecate in sacred places — on the altars of God and on the law — and expect God to pack our faeces.

Nevertheless, the issue is controversial. You see, in the Bible, there was a time the church was growing so fast and the believers were living as one community. They shared their food and resources in common. Problems came up. The Apostles who were both the spiritual and administrative heads of the church were concerned. However, they soon found that their administrative duties were beginning to take a toll on their spiritual and primary responsibilities. What was their resolve? They chose to let other men handle the administrative duties, while they would focus on their spiritual roles. In actual fact, the very duties the Apostles declined and handed over to deacons were even the administrative duties of the church. (See Acts of Apostles ch. 6 vs. 2 – in the Holy Bible). How much more then should a pastor not avoid being encumbered with the administrative duties of the nation or of a political party? Again, I must say, that is my personal opinion of what the Bible says, other people may have a different opinion but I do not seek to press the matter further.

That particular pastor is a man I personally respect and like. I like his reasoning. I like his eloquence and I have nothing at all against him. I believe in him. My only reservation about him is this matter in Acts 6: 2, and if you are not a Christian, it doesn't concern you. It's an internal affair within the Christendom.

However, if I was asked, I would say let pastors and imams and other religious leaders maintain political neutrality in public. That is where God stands, I believe, and there I stand.

On my Facebook profile[6] – long before I got the idea about writing this book – in the space for me to indicate my political views, I had written that *"Well, I should be politically neutral but I have more friends in the PDP than other parties"*. As I prepare to publish this book, I thought about pulling that off my Facebook profile because I wouldn't like to have that misconstrued. In the long run, I decided to leave it unchanged. Someone might read that tomorrow and interpret it as an endorsement of the PDP. Well, that is just a matter of fact and it's open to debate. The truth is that the PDP is the country's largest party. If I am politically neutral and take all politicians as my friends, leaving no one out, naturally then, I will have more friends in the PDP than in the other parties. This is what that profile comment means and no further meaning is intended. If by tomorrow any other party becomes bigger than the PDP, automatically, I will have more friends in that other party than the PDP because my disposition is to take all as friends. It is simple arithmetic and does not determine who I will vote for or not in the approaching elections. I have taken my stand where God stands – "he who rules over men must be just".

---

[6] http://www.facebook.com/oyetomi

Chapter 2

God Himself Has Done The Zoning

God has already zoned Presidency, Kaduna governorship – Yakowa
- The Punch newspaper, 27 Nov 2010

Federal Character

When we were kids, we had birthday parties here and there. Usually there would be cakes to share after the celebrants had blown out the candles. Everyone would want a piece of the cake. However small the cake might be, it had to be severally divided so that it could go round.

Then we would have music. About 8 of us would be made to dance around 7 seats. Then the music would be abruptly stopped, and everyone would try to claim a seat immediately; whoever didn't get a seat lost out. Then, one seat would be removed and the remaining 7 kids would have to dance round 6 seats. The game would go on and on, until only one winner emerged. Hmmn. Sweet memories. Kids' play.

Why do I still remember all these stuff? Possibly because there is a child inside that has refused to grow up. The greater truth, however, is that the way government is run at all levels in this country always remind me of those funny children games. We talk about "the national cake" – or as BJ and his friends used to call it "the national *moin-moin*" – and everyone wants to eat a piece of it without actively seeking to contribute to how it is baked and preserved. Please, can we try and grow up?

The Nigerian common sense is that "*if it is not equal, then it is not fair*". As a matter of fact, sometimes if things are equal, the situation becomes unfair. Why are your fingers not of equal length and thickness?

Our nation has taken the issue of equality too far. We already have a Senate that has equal representation from all the states, yet our constitution require that the

17

Federal Cabinet must have at least a minister appointed from each state. What's the use? So, that each state can have a share of the "national *moin-moin*". We have used this dormant idea of maintaining "federal character" to create a lot of unnecessary problems. For example, if we have a president who had removed, say, his Minister of Justice, and knows a particular highly intelligent and competent person from a different ethnicity that he could appoint to fill that post, the president may be unable to appoint that person simply because the available ministerial "slot" belongs to a particular state. He would have to shuffle around the cabinet in other to bring the competent person on board. Why the hassle?

Zoning

Dancing round the seats and wanting a piece of the cake, not too bad. It has only helped to reduce governance into mere kids' play. Somehow – anyhow – that kids' play found its way to the centre of our politics in the recent past. Of a truth, some parts of the country have produced more heads of state for the country than others. In terms of number of heads of state and the total length of years they have stayed in office, the North has ruled this country far more than the South. However, I do not see any particular problem with that.

See, our country copied the form of government that is not the best for us. We should have stayed with the parliamentary system thrust upon us by the colonial governments. Rather, because of the glamour and success of the American style of democracy, we copied their form of government without copying their method of funding and maintaining that model of government.

There is this joke I have often heard about "copyrights". *Dem go talk say "no problem about copying anything, so far you copy it right. That is copyright"*. (Funny). Yet we have not managed to "copy it right" as a nation.

For instance, the Americans we copied do not often use this method of "State of Origin" that we use. They use "State of Residence". So, if a man of Hausa descent were born in Ibadan and has lived in Ibadan for the 52 years of his life, he would not be prevented from seeking to become the Governor of Oyo State – I mean if it were the American method. Here, it's different. People would mockingly tell him, *"come and point out your forefathers' houses here to us. Go and sit down. You are a foreigner."*

Then when it's time for census, the man will also pack his household and travel to Kano to his ancestral home and be counted there, only to return to Ibadan after the census. Why? Because the Federal Government shares some part of the "national cake" according to the population of the area. He travels to his "home state" at census so as to boost the share of the national cake that would go to that state.

I am amused every time some big politicians travel to their ancestral villages to register as voters and also vote from there while for most of their lifetime they have been based elsewhere. All these show that our country lacks unity. The way to unite the country, however, is not by "sharing the national cake" and dancing round dwindling resources.

Do you know that in the United States, 2 particular states – the States of Ohio and Virginia – have produced more presidents than the other states? Obama is America's 44th President. Of the previous 43 presidents, 15 came from the States of Ohio and Virginia only, whereas America has 52 states[7]. The two states are in the same region. In fact, there is only one state – West Virginia – separating them. Do you know that the eastern part of the US has produced more presidents than the western part? Do you know that these facts have not led them into making any zoning arrangements in the over

Rather, because of the glamour and success of the American style of democracy, we copied their form of government without copying their method of funding and maintaining that model of government.

---

[7] http://www.whitehouse.gov/about/presidents/

200 years of their democracy? Because democracy out there is not about sharing the national cake as we have it here. (Not that they don't share the cake, though. It's just that they have a civilised manner of doing so.)

So, why all the ado about kicking the seat of the president back and forth between the North and the South? If we know that we cannot copy the spirit and thinking of the Americans, why then do we copy their form of government? The fact is that the success of the American pattern of democracy is not rooted in the form; it is rooted in the principles – the ideologies. Our error lies in the fact that we copied their form without copying their ideologies.

Born To Rule

. . . it would seem that the various political offices available in Nigeria are avenues for undue advantages of various sorts. If it were not so, we won't bother about where the president hails from

Every state in Nigeria has an official slogan. Lagos is "Centre of Excellence", Ekiti is "Fountain of Knowledge", a particular state from the North once featured the "born to rule" slogan. Born to rule? Yeah. Don't worry, the "rule" is not defined.

I have often heard many southerners resenting the fact that the northerners have the idea that they are born to rule this country. Why not, if not? I don't care if the North always produces the president, or if it were the South for that matter. The only question I would ask is "how knowledgeable, insightful and just, is the person who is being elected as president?"

The way we go about it, it would seem that the various political offices available in Nigeria are avenues for undue advantages of various sorts. If it were not so, we won't bother about where the president hails from. On the contrary, we have often believed that if the president is from the North, he would

20

give a bigger share of the national cake to the North, or if the president is from the South, he would do the same for the South. In a sense, we do not even see that as corruption, and that is why the country does not appear to grow at all.

In a true democracy, no one is born to rule. Becoming president or governor should not be the birth right of any particular person or people; it should be open to all and for all and should be fairly contested, not zoned.

Unconstitutional Constitutions

The PDP held its presidential primaries early in the year. It was broadcast live on TV. I watched and listened as one of the aspirants described herself as "zoning neutraliser". Another candidate vehemently defended the provisions allegedly made in the PDP constitution for rotating the office of the president between the North and the South. I don't seem to comprehend that. What legal rights do any particular party have to zone the office of the president of the Federal Republic to a particular region? Ideally, a party can only zone the office of the president or chairman of its own party and not that of the country.

I would opine that in the future, we should advocate that the electoral laws of this country should require that the constitution of political parties must be passed by a body of benchers to determine that such constitutions are not at variance with the constitution of the Federal Republic before licences are granted to such parties. Parties already licensed should also have their licences reviewed according to that provision. It would save the nation from a lot of unnecessary feuds and rancour and would ensure that only the best minds attain to the highest office.

Even the Constitution Itself

The 1999 Constitution was given to us by a military decree. The majority of the people had no input. The recent amendments were done by the ruling class without a mass referendum on some sensitive issues and without any sovereign national conference for the review of the constitution. Yet, we call it democracy. Of course, it really isn't.

True democracy begins when power shifts to the people, but power will not shift to the people unless it begins from a sovereign national conference for creating a new constitution.

Our Nobel Laureate, Prof. Wole Soyinka, has consistently canvassed for a sovereign national conference over the years. His voice has gone unheeded over and over again. For me, I always try to listen very carefully when highly intelligent people speak. Well, fellow Nigerians, I can only wish you good luck. If we continue with the ridiculous manner we have been running the country, our country with some luck might never collapse but it would simply never progress.

To Defend Her Unity

Nigerians are lucky, we have a richly-worded national anthem and in addition, a well-crafted national pledge. "*I pledge to Nigeria my country, to be faithful, loyal and honest . . . to defend her unity and uphold her honour and glory . . .*". What a noble declaration! However, come to think of it; what unity do we have in the first place? Of course, it is true we are one country, but it is not true that we are a united country. The very people who lead us to pledge to "defend the unity" of the country are the same people who turn around to demand that the presidency or some offices be zoned to a particular region.

We do often forget the fact that this country was not one country from the very beginning. It was a merger of the North and the South. When in 1914, Sir Frederick Luggard amalgamated the separate protectorates of Southern and Northern Nigeria, he presumably did not understand African thinking. Such mergers may work where people don't care who your father is, or where you were born. What he did to our lands and nations in 1914 was to join people that were not in courtship in a matrimony – just for the convenience of his own administration and the foreign authorities that sent him here. Today, that marriage is nearly 100 years old, yet it is a matter of constant rancour and acrimony.

You think Nigeria is 50 years old? Wrong. Nigeria is actually 97 years old. The country was born when the North and the South were merged in 1914. The 50 years that was recently celebrated was for the years since independent governance.

I like unity and diversity. I like to see a blend of different customs and cultures. I always like to hear different languages. It is a blessing that we are so many and

22

so diverse. However, as in any marriage, the inherent individual human rights of each partner must be respected and preserved. Every now and then, marriages are dissolved for reasons of spousal abuse. As it applies to marriages between individuals, it equally applies to marriages between nations and cultures.

Marital Assault and Divorce

Some men are always aggressive, they can never be pleased. They seem to always wait for the slightest provocations before they strike. There are families where the wife earns more money than the husband, yet the husband after forcibly taking the resources of the wife, would still recourse to beating her blue and black; it is unfair. I would not want to draw a parallel between that picture and how it appears between some African nations that were merged at the whims of the colonial governments.

Notwithstanding, as I was preparing this book for publication, an African country that has a similar demographic pattern to that of Nigeria went into referendum to determine whether they should split or remain as one country. That country is Sudan – with a predominantly Moslem north and a predominantly Christian and oil-rich south – just like Nigeria. It was plagued by wars and battles aggravated by emphasis on their differences.

It is fantastic that our own country has always managed to overcome the tensions caused by our differences and contrived to defend her territorial integrity all these years (except for giving away Bakassi peninsula). Yet every time the argument comes up that the presidency should be zoned to a particular region or not; it makes me sick to the bones.

Don't get me wrong, I'm not against the idea of a rotational presidency. However, a rotational presidency would mean that we would have to first reduce the powers of the central federal government and have stronger regional governments. Thus, the real governments would be the regional premiership and the central government would be largely ceremonial. To speak in terms of zoning, therefore, is to seek the devolution of powers of the central federal government. It's not completely a bad idea. What would be bad is for one particular party to impose the provisions of its own constitution upon the nation. If that party is convinced that zoning or rotating the presidency between the

North and the South is the best arrangement, then the party would have to call other parties into dialogue and jointly present the idea before the nation so that it could be incorporated into the constitution of the Federal Republic.

Whatsoever God Has Joined Together

A friend once told me a story. There was this man who attempted to kill his wife and use her for "blood money" rituals. She luckily escaped. Thereafter, she went for counselling and her pastor made her understand that *"whatsoever God has joined together, let no man put asunder. You have to be a good believer and obey the word of God. You can't divorce him"*. Ehhhh! Indeed? Even after the man has attempted to take the life of the woman and already wants her dead? Didn't they sign *"till death do us part"*? Of course, as far as the man is concerned, the woman was better dead than alive. In fact, he had already killed her in his thoughts.

I believe in the sacredness of marriage. I mean the marriage also between the North and the South of this country. But if the South ever insists on having a southern president, and the North ever insists on having a northern president, then, each side might just as well have its own president and its own territory as a matter of course. I believe it was God who through Luggard joined us together – that we may become one. However, if after 97 years we are yet to become one, then each region might as well go its own way. That's the way I see it. Don't get me wrong, I prefer that the country should maintain her present territorial integrity. Staying together means, however, that we should stop being sentimental about ethnicity and religion.

The idea of zoning has the implication that northern Christians will never be presidents of this country and neither would southern Moslems. We had a Christian from the South as president from 1999 to 2007. If he had handed over to a Christian from the North and that person remains in office for 8 years, you would begin to hear murmurs that *"it's only the Christians that are ruling this country. It's unfair"*. If a Moslem from the North rules for 8 years and hands over to a Moslem from the South, there would be murmurs that *"only the Moslems are ruling this country"*. If we go by the kind of zoning arrangement that tosses the presidency from the north to the south back and forth, eventually, all we shall have in this country would be a system of 8 years of rule by a Christian from the

South, and 8 years of rule by a Moslem from the North in a perpetual circle. Who would that hurt? No one, really. It would only mean that we won't ever stop seeing ourselves as Northerners and Southerners or Christians and Moslems and true unity will ever evade us. How long shall we continue to see ourselves only in terms of race and religion? And more importantly, how long shall the presidency continue to be a "rule" rather than an "administration"?

God Himself Has Done The Zoning

Patrick Yakowa, the incumbent governor of Kaduna state was not pushing to become a governor. He was a deputy governor. Then, luck smiled on him. His then boss, Mohammed Sambo, became Vice-President, and Patrick automatically became the governor.

He was answering questions from journalists about the PDP zoning arrangements and was quoted as saying "*God has already zoned Presidency*". Hmnn.

Late President Y'aradua passed on after a protracted illness. He had become president after OBJ's 8 years' administration. OBJ is from the South, and Y'aradua was from the North. Some old men – fathers and grandfathers, in fact – were still enjoying the games of dancing round the chairs and getting a piece of the cake. They believed it was now the turn of the North to rule and control the national cake. *Haba*. But then, tragedy struck and Y'aradua passed on. Then, the Presidency was thrust upon Goodluck Jonathan by the Constitution. If some people had their way, they won't have allowed Jonathan to take that seat – like kids, they would have told him "*get up from that seat. It's our seat. It's still our turn to sit on it . . . I will tell your daddy, I will tell teacher.*" Kids. I wonder why some people lack serious activities that could keep them busy.

If some people had their way, they won't have allowed Jonathan to take that seat – like kids, they would have told him "get up from that seat. It's our seat. It's still our turn to sit on it

25

But their eyes are fixated on the "national cake". It's all about eating. No, not food – money, actually. If you listen well to the average Nigerians, they always talk about *dem*. "*Dem siddon there dey chop moni*". "*Dem dey eat money*".

However, as fate would have it, Y'aradua died of natural causes. In the same year, the President of Poland had died in a plane crash. Sadly. We must thank God that Y'aradua did not die in a plane crash. Had it been that he died in a plane crash, some folks who believe that "*it's still our turn to sit on that seat*" may have begun to insinuate that it was a foul play engineered to take "their seat" from "them". But no one took their seat from them. It was natural – an act of God. A presidency that was purportedly "zoned" to the North, was re-zoned by an act of God to the South. Common, these are not my original sentiments – I quote Governor Yakowa, a Northerner, "*God has already zoned Presidency*".[8]

You know what? God didn't do it as "zoning" or "re-zoning". God was just showing through his act that there shouldn't be zoning in the first place. And God was showing this because the constitution of the Federal Republic did not say anything about zoning of the office of the President of the Federal Republic. God being just and fair therefore would make us see that once we recognise the constitution of the Federal Republic as the supreme law of our land, every other constitution must be subservient to the constitution of the Federal Republic. That's God's own "zoning", I believe.

---

[8] The Punch, 27 November 2010

Chapter 3

I Dey Laugh O

2011: Obasanjo laughs at Atiku's emergence as consensus aspirant
- The Punch, 26 November 2010

I Dey Laugh O

I knew it. I knew that the press would be looking out for Obasaanjo to comment on the emergence of his former deputy, erstwhile vice-president Atiku Abubakar, as the consensus aspirant of factions within the PDP that were clamouring for zoning the presidency to the North.

Obasanjo and the press have a way with one another that would seem to be a game of hide and seek. The press seem to have formed the habit of asking OBJ very tricky questions and then interpreting his answers as they deem fit while it would seem that Obasanjo too is always trying to avoid speaking directly with the press. I like the language used in the Punch article on 26 November 2010. The writer stated that journalists "accosted" Obasanjo at the State House and the latter had initially declined to comment but "after some prodding", said "*I dey laugh o*" and then proceeded to laugh. (Don't ask why I am always taking my news pieces from the Punch – it just happens to be the newspaper I buy most often). I did look up the dictionary meaning of the word "accosted" to be sure I was not getting it wrong. That's not the material point, anyway.

When I saw the headlines, I wondered if Obasanjo was underestimating Atiku or simply found the whole idea of a consensus aspirant laughable. For me, I knew that each of the four aspirants that were negotiating for a consensus aspirant among themselves was a formidable contestant for the PDP ticket for the presidential election. There was former military president, Ibrahim Babangida; former national security adviser, Aliyu Gusau, incumbent Kwara state governor and son of the "strong man" of Kwara politics, Bukola Saraki as well as Atiku Abubakar. They had formed themselves into an alliance known as the Northern Political Leaders' Forum, NPLF.

One of the major arguments of the NPLF was the issue of zoning the presidency to the North. In the previous chapter, I have already spoken my mind about "zoning" and do not need to repeat it here. And that was not just my mind – even former head of state Muhammadu Buhari and former Chairman of the Economic and Financial Crimes Commission, Nuhu Ribadu, both of whom are now seeking to be elected as president of the country both described "zoning" as "a PDP affair". Of course, both of them are Northerners, if you will have it, but I like the fact that they did not present themselves under that identity. Rather, they presented themselves as nationalists, as far as zoning is concerned. As a person, I always find it "laughable" when anyone who seeks to head the whole country presents himself or herself as a representative of just one section of the country.

For many people, they can't ever see themselves as simply Nigerians without breaking it down to ethnicity. I know a lot of folks around here who spoke very favourably about Jonathan until certain people from the southwest accepted party nominations as vice-presidential candidates. It became clearer to me that the reason they were initially supporting Jonathan was simply because they saw him as a "southerner". And the moment they got someone else from their "own side" of the South aspiring to become vice-president, the sentiment became *"Ehn, Yoruba a tubo rowo mu"* – *"a Yoruba man will become No.2 citizen, which would be better for the Yoruba nation than it would otherwise be under Jonathan"*. If I didn't grow up here, I would have been surprised. Such thinking is not just ridiculous, it is also disgusting.

Sectionalism and tribalism are immature and uncivil. Well, I have already laughed all I could about the "zoning" arguments. The only thing I am doing now is trying to make up my mind who to vote for in April or whether I should eventually "neutralise" my vote. Really, considering the great effort I have already put into getting myself distracted from my usual orientation to queue for over two hours, just to register as a voter, and then also spending much time and energy writing this book, I would like to follow through and not kill my vote. I am at least 85% sure, though, that I will be voting. Common, don't be pessimistic about me – 85% is an excellent mark. In the university, we give students who have at least a 70% score an 'A' – the highest possible grade. If the police would guarantee that security would not be kids' play during the elections and that voters would not lose their limbs trying to vote and assure us that it has taken care of the threat of MEND (the Movement for the Emancipation of the Niger Delta) to turn polling booths into bombing booths, then you can bet I would be definitely voting. 100% sure. For now, I am waiting for the campaigns to pause and let's have some good debates from the candidates – it's curious that we are less than 1 month to the elections and there has not been any serious debate between the presidential candidates. That's all that is reviving my laughter at this time – "*I still dey laugh o*". Do you mean that people are simply planning to vote on the basis of the names they like, what ethnicity the candidates belong to, and yet we expect to see positive changes? That's laughable.

Obasanjo is our problem. Really?
I said it earlier, Nigeria is a crazy country. We have the problems of both leadership and followership. Somehow, it seems that good leadership and good followership are mutually exclusive in this country. When the leaders are ready to progress, the followers are not, and vice-versa.

Most of us grow up blaming "the government" for all our woes. In fact, some get so used to it that even when they get into government, they still blame "the government" without realising that they have also become part of it. I have been at a lecture delivered by a top government functionary from Abuja and one of his recommendations was that "*the government should increase the funding for this sector*". I wondered what he meant by that.

When the military ruled, we would say the military were the problems. "*If only the military would retreat to their barracks, face their professional duties and stop interfering in politics, everything would be well. We would live in luxury. Nigeria would become Utopia.*" Well, the military handed over to civilians nearly 12 years ago but we have not arrived at that Nigerian Dream yet.

As luck would have it, the president that came on board to hold the reins in 1999 *is* in fact a retired general. Back then, I would often concur when people

29

said he still had some of the "soldier blood" in him – "once a soldier, always a soldier". Was he the best for the nation? Yes, probably, if you would have it.

Obasanjo having fought for the territorial integrity of the nation during the Nigerian civil war is a man who believes that the unity of the country is sacrosanct. No matter what we go through, whether militants are blowing up the Niger Delta, or Fulani herdsmen are in endless skirmishes with crop farmers, or Jos North is sitting on barrels of gunpowder, in so far as we contrive to "keep the country together", it is worth celebrating as far as Obasanjo is concerned. What more can I say? See, Baba, I understand what it means to you, sir. I know that when a man has risked life and limbs to preserve a treasure, he would not tolerate anyone who trivialises it. The only problem here is that when we who never witnessed the war or fought in it sing *"the labours of our heroes past shall never be in vain"* in the national anthem, it sounds to us as just some vague melody. We have no idea what those bloody *"labours"* were; or rather what those *"heroes"* who paid with their lives to keep the country together faced in the war. All that matters to us are *"good roads, electricity, better education . . . zoning the knife that cuts national cake"*. It's not our fault. However, I think we can still manage to ensure that the *"labours of our heroes past"* are not in vain without sacrificing any of our present basic and urgent needs.

> I said it earlier, Nigeria is a crazy country. We have the problems of both leadership and followership. Somehow, it seems that good leadership and good followership are mutually exclusive in this country.

President Obasanjo is a lucky man. He had been caught and kept in the barn by "the leopard". "The leopard" passed on . . . it was rumoured that it was "an apple" . . . and Obasanjo was freed. He came from prison to power, and such a great power it was. Then came the blessings too. No sooner had he become president that oil prices began to rise again. Crude oil prices were about $18 per barrel when Obasanjo became president in 1999 but when he was leaving office in 2007 oil prices had climbed to about $78 per barrel. His entire 8 years in power was a period of oil boom, averagely. I remember that during his first term, as civilian president, he would usually say "*I see hope*". Many of us saw that "hope" too. However, I wonder why he talked less about it during his second term and we also stopped seeing it. I can't be sure now which came first, whether it was because he stopped talking about the hope that made us lose sight of it, or whether it was because we lost sight of it that made him stop talking about it.

I don't want to unnecessarily stretch the length of this book, so I will be silent on some issues – many issues, actually. But I remember I used to have some wayward neighbours. The four kids were often saucy and erratic. Every now and then, you would hear them praising their parents. That is, whenever their parents "*settle*" them. Their parents were at such times "*the best parents on earth*". Those very kids would turn around to *yab* their parents at any time things went slightly tough for the family. Spoilt children. I used to wonder if those kids knew that their parents were still the same whether the family economy boomed or dwindled.

Take it or leave it, Obasanjo made many positive contributions to the nation during his 8 years in office. Whether he allowed us or not to empty the pot and eat enough to quench our hunger – like the four kids of my erstwhile neighbour would often like to do – is a different argument entirely. But I can count many of the achievements of his administration – relentless pursuit of our nation's exit from the Paris Club and the attendant debt cancellation was one. Establishing the Economic and Financial Crimes Commission, which has made at least one of the present presidential candidates popular is another. He had a habit of choosing very brilliant and serious-minded technocrats as his ministers and

> *I don't want to unnecessarily stretch the length of this book, so I will be silent on some issues – many issues, actually.*

advisers. He renovated and acquired additional equipment for the nation's teaching hospitals; he reformed the pension scheme of the Federal Civil Service; he made several increases in salaries and wages. These are just to mention a few.

Okay, I get it. You would like me to say some stuff. See, it's not decorous to say in public everything that is on one's mind. (And a book is in fact a "public place", in case you never thought of it as such). I remember this joke about a man who was brought to the magistrate over an accusation. The prosecution threatened to produce 5 people who saw him do the act. The accused man retorted that he too could produce at least 500 people who did not see him do the act. You get the point? For everything a man manages to do, it is possible to list 100 things he did not do. But in this case, whether he had the capability to do them is open to debate. I will leave it at that.

> . . . we can still manage to ensure that the "labours of our heroes past" are not in vain without sacrificing any of our present basic and urgent needs.

Actually, I know a lot of people who believe that Obasanjo "imposed" Y'aradua on the nation and also foreknew the fact that Y'aradua's health might not last him through his first term. Some even said he chose Jonathan as Y'aradua's deputy so that Jonathan could succeed Y'aradua and he could perpetuate his [Obasanjo's] influence on the affairs of the nation. As far as such people are concerned, Obasanjo is still the one in power until now. Usually, I find such sentiments laughable. No doubt, Obasanjo has influence in the government of the day. He is after all the incumbent Chairman of the Board of Trustees of the PDP, the party governing the most states in the country and with the largest proportion of the national assembly, and he also has a constitutional role as member of the Council of State. However, that does not make the incumbent president his stooge. I don't have to dwell on that. Read the newspapers, and analyse.

Last December, as we were preparing to attend the "cross over night" service in church, a friend called me about a rumour that Obasanjo had died. He wanted me to search the internet and confirm. I called a friend in Abeokuta to help me find out. A student was with me when I made the call. The student said, "*Ah, if that's true, it means that God is about to intervene in the affairs of this country*". I was a little startled. I told him, "*Don't speak that way. I don't expect such from an educated fellow like you. See, the heavens are God's but the earth he has given to the children of men*", I was quoting the Bible. The student insisted that "*Obasanjo is one of our greatest problems in this country. If it's true that he's dead, ah, the politics of 2011 will change God is at work!*". He was so excited about it. I was baffled. When we returned from church, it was settled that Obasanjo had not died. It was an empty rumour. I asked the student, "*So, now that Obasanjo is not dead, does it mean that God is no longer having hands in the affairs of the country?*". He was speechless.

> No doubt, Obasanjo has influence in the government of the day. He is after all the incumbent Chairman of the Board of Trustees of the PDP, . . .

Philanthropist or Miser?

I mentioned earlier that Nigerian leaders and followers don't trust one another. This informs why the average Nigerian will hardly have anything good to say about the leaders, especially those who have left office. When you are in office, they might speak well about you – to your face – although they would say a lot of damaging things behind you. But when you leave office, you hardly get any praise. All you would be remembered for are things they expected you to do but you did not, or could not, do. Whatever positive things you did would fade out of their minds.

If you asked the average Nigerians about Obasanjo's personality, probably one of the first things they would tell you is that "the man is a miser". They would say it so personally that you would think that they once lived next door to him. Then, you will also hear that *"he is too sure of himself and feels he is the only one that can run the affairs of the country. He wanted a third term"*.

I can't recollect in details those third-term episodes any more but I don't think that either Obasanjo or any of his closest aides or ministers publicly discussed the third term issue while he was in office. The issue was raised in the National Assembly and also died in the National Assembly. The popular opinion, though, was that he had his invisible hands at work in the National Assembly to push his interests towards a third term in office.

Personally, I do not speak in definite terms concerning things of which I am not certain. I will leave the issue about the dead "third term agenda" to those who claim to have the facts and to the conscience of both the nation and the former president.

However, I would say this, I have had two personal encounters with Obasanjo and these gave me a perspective of him that is quite different from what we usually hear from the common man on the streets.

In 2007 after Obasanjo left office, I read in the newspapers that journalists had questioned him on why he chose to enrol for a degree in Theology at the National Open University of Nigeria, NOUN. He had responded that he enrolled because he wanted to know more about God. Okay, I sent him a copy of my book ***Does God Truly Exist?*** and explained it might help him in his quest to know more of God. I was surprised weeks later when I received a letter personally signed by him thanking me for the book and mentioning to me that the studies at the NOUN had been worth his while and concluding that "truly God exists indeed". You know what? I took that as an act of humility. After all, I had given out copies of the book *gratis* to many other people who never bothered to say "thank you". Some asked their secretaries to write and acknowledge my gesture. Many did not acknowledge the gift at all – and such people do not even have half as much commitments and accomplishments as

Obasanjo. Yet they probably felt too busy, or too important, to write a "thank you" letter.

And then there was 2008. I was planning to attend a course which would cost me about $10,000 and needed to raise another sum for a project. I didn't have the funds. I made a short list of people whom I felt might be able to assist. Philanthropists. Bishops. Pastors. I wrote to Obasanjo as well. I made follow up calls and visits to people I had written to. I was not allowed to see many of them. They were too busy. I went to Abeokuta. I enquired if I could see Obasanjo. I was told he would be travelling out the following morning but would be back within a week. There would be only two weeks left before the course I was meant to attend. When Obasanjo returned to the country, I spoke with one of his aides and he put me on the visitors' list. I met Obasanjo for a very brief moment. He didn't speak much. He gave me $1000. The aide explained to me that "Baba felt you had support from other sources as well". But indeed, there were no other sources. Indeed if I had 9 other people like Obasanjo at that time each giving me $1000, I would have been able to pay for the course! But no, there were none. Even the philanthropists did not respond to my request. They didn't even take the courtesy to ask their secretaries to write back, even if it would be something like "sorry, we can't help you at this time". They just kept quiet. Afterwards, I read in the newspapers an interview in which a philanthropist, a popular SAN based in Ibadan, mentioned that the difference between him and Obasanjo is that "*Obasanjo is a miser*" – quote and unquote. I wondered what it means to be a miser. I mean, "the miser" gave me a thousand dollars – to a man he never knew personally and was meeting for the first time – whereas the philanthropist gave me absolutely nothing!

See, I have mentioned that encounter with Obasanjo to some of my friends who said to me, "oh oh, he has bought your conscience. You speak well about him now because he gave you $1000". Not exactly. What's a thousand dollars? I'm not a millionaire but I also have a "givers' attitude". Giving, and especially to strangers and those who would not be able to pay you back is a principle I have learnt from the Bible and do practise. In the year that Obasanjo gave me $1000, I had also given out more than $1000 cumulatively for that year within the limits of my incomes. So, it's not an issue about selling my conscience for $1000. The basic truth is that the man is not the "miser" and "demon" (or "*ebora*") that we are often told he is. He may have made his mistakes. He may have made decisions that were very costly to the nation. But overall I would give him a pass mark. Character-wise, he is much better than the average Nigerian. Take it or leave it.

Why am I bringing this up here? I'm bringing it up for two simple reasons. One, to highlight the fact that we Nigerians seem to act on the impulse of emotions rather than reason and seem to gullibly believe every unreasonable thing said about our leaders. Second, we also seem to be easily fooled by the "kind acts" of many so-called philanthropists that we often do not see their selfish ulterior motives.

> *. . . we Nigerians seem to act on the impulse of emotions rather than reason and seem to gullibly believe every unreasonable thing said about our leaders.*

There is a man who had an NGO in his name. I will rather call it 123 Foundation. He was using trucks to deliver water to villages across his state. He claimed to have a passion for the suffering the people were facing in terms of potable water. At a particular time, he even distributed kerosene for their cooking stoves. Then he became the governor of his state. He is no longer the governor of that state now. And also there doesn't seem to be so much activity being done by 123 Foundation. That's just an example. In hindsight, I would think he founded 123 Foundation in order to win the affection and votes of his people. We see a lot of it during election years. Scholarships and bursaries are launched by some wealthy aspirants for public office. Greek gifts. Those are the stuff that are ruining the correct functionality of the country today. I wonder why people don't see through the acts of these fake philanthropists and go on to vote for them with eyes wide shut!

Drunk drivers steering the nation?

Please kindly don't mind the fact that I seem to have devoted most of this chapter to talking about Obasanjo. I am doing it for a reason. It's not about him.

36

It's about you and I. It's about how we reason and how we make our choices, and how we perceive our leaders.

If you are the aggressive type, I am the kind of person you will not normally like because my disposition is that every person has certain good qualities, whereas most Nigerians often speak in absolute terms. Most Nigerians would simply say that "our leaders are bad. They are only there to eat money". Or, they would say, "that man is a good man". Practically, there are no good or bad persons. There are only good and bad decisions (or, indecisions), or good and bad actions.

So, when you talk about Babangida, Obasanjo, Atiku, Jonathan, Ribadu, Shekarau, Buhari, Bakare, Utomi, Okotie, etc. Are they good people? Yes, they are – just like you. Are they bad people? Yes, they are – just like you. The categorisation of someone as either good or bad will depend on your own perceptions and the limits of your understanding.

Having travelled in public buses many times, I can say a few things about the attitudes of backseat passengers. When a bus suddenly veers off its lane and sharply returns to it, there will be shouts and screams. *"Mr. Driver, are you sleeping? Are you drunk?!!!"*. Backseat passengers do not often see what the driver had suddenly avoided. And they don't trust the driver's judgment enough to believe he was doing the right thing. Driving under influence is not practically a crime in Nigeria – it's an egoistic thing. Most drivers of public transport vehicles usually take substances and see it as "normal". Even the general public seem to accept is as "normal". You get to the bus terminals and can hardly see a complete gentleman who works as a driver. Most of them drink and dope and boast about it. That idea seems to be transferred into our governance. We don't trust the men that steer the wheels of the nation. Most of

> *We don't trust the men that steer the wheels of the nation. Most of our leaders seem to be power-drunk and greed-intoxicated.*

37

our leaders seem to be power-drunk and greed-intoxicated. *"It's normal"*. So, "the masses" are often wary of even well-meaning actions on the part of the government. We can't ever trust the government enough over anything.

The Government is not doing anything.

During the Abacha years, a friend and I were watching the NTA Network News. Abacha had just inaugurated the Aluminium Smelter Company of Nigeria. I commented that *"I like this. That's a good thing Abacha has done"*. My friend protested, *"What do you mean? The guy is a moron. He's not doing anything. People are suffering"*. I told him, *"Well, no matter what, he is still our Head of State, and why call him a moron?. After all, he is more intelligent than you"*. My friend took offence at that last statement. He warned me, *"Hey, Mr. Man, watch it. Don't insult me!"* I wondered what was insulting in telling a young undergraduate that the then Head of State, a general in the army, who had passed through the National Institute for Policy and Strategic Studies, and had been trained overseas, was more intelligent than him. His attitude is reflective of the attitude of most of us. We always have better ideas than the government. Yet most of those "better ideas" end up as screams, grumbling, and murmuring, on the back seats. As it turned out, that friend of mine became a local government councillor in 1999. I am yet to see him demonstrate his better-than-Abacha's intelligence since he also became part of the government.

Abacha is best remembered today for allegedly looting the national treasury. Yet this doesn't mean that as Head of State, *"he didn't do anything"*. The states created during his regime still exist till today. The Petroleum Trust Fund he established made considerable interventions in different sectors of the society. I am not in position to answer whether the PTF was a successful venture while it lasted. But we are fortunate that the man Abacha appointed to head the PTF back then is still alive today and is one of those running for the office of the president presently. I believe this man would not agree with my dear friend that *"Abacha didn't do anything when he was president"*. And of course, it would be equally unfair to this other noble man to say, *"You served in the government that looted the nation"*. However, many Nigerians don't see it that way. To them, *"Babangida didn't do anything. Abacha didn't do anything. Obasanjo didn't do anything"*. How so?

38

Forget about the military era. Let's talk about 1999 to date. You mean Obasanjo didn't do anything at all? Really? What about all the reforms he initiated while in office? The monetisation policy? National debt reduction? Pension reforms? Do you remember that, before Obasanjo, Federal Government workers used to wait nearly two full years before they got their retirement gratuities and first pensions? Do you realise that now most of them get their retirement benefits almost as soon as they leave office due to the reforms Obasanjo initiated? Do you know that the purchasing power of most civil servants increased considerably under Obasanjo? Do you see that his administration initiated far-reaching reforms in the banking and telecoms sector?

Go out in the streets, and ask if anyone remembers that the Obasanjo administration invested 100 million Euros in the modernisation and equipment of the 8 largest teaching hospitals across the country. The answer you will get is, *"No. Was there ever anything of that sort? We can't remember that. We are not talking about that. What we are talking about is that there is no water. No electricity. No good roads. Obasanjo didn't do anything"*. Even one of the leading presidential aspirants said, *"the party that has ruled the country since 1999 has done nothing in 12 years"*. I underlined the word "nothing". Excuse me, most times, I like being exact. There is a difference between "has not done enough" or "has not done as we expected" and "has done nothing". I am not trying to defend or justify the government. I, too, often criticise the government and ask questions and it is not every policy of the government I agree with and neither am I completely satisfied with the level of performance of the various tiers of the government. Yet, I wouldn't say "the government has done nothing" because that would not be correct – whether logically, politically or religiously.

I Demand Absolute Loyalty

Don't forget I started this chapter by laughing. Unlike Obasanjo, I was not laughing at the emergence of Atiku as the consensus candidate. But then I did laugh when on January 13, I watched the live broadcast of the PDP presidential primaries. No, I didn't laugh when Atiku lost the primaries or because of that. I laughed when Jonathan came to the podium, briefly highlighted the notable achievements of his brief administration and almost angrily demanded rhetorically "what are you talking about?", apparently in response to Aitku who had insinuated (or, stated – if you prefer) that the Jonathan administration *"has done nothing in 8 months*". I laughed because even leaders seem to have joined "the masses" in making a lot of politically incorrect statements.

Earlier, Atiku had talked about zoning and also tried to discredit Jonathan's performance in office. As the camera briefly shifted to Obasanjo – my thoughts drifted back to the Obasanjo-Atiku administration. I briefly remembered when it was reported in the papers that Obasanjo had said "I demand absolute loyalty" and the papers interpreted it to mean a reference to questioning Atiku's loyalty. Back then, I joked that Baba still carries the military idea of absolute loyalty. I would say, "You can't get that in a world of politics".

See, if there is any of the politicians from the North that I like, it would be Atiku. Why? Because of his drive and tenacity. I like people who are determined in their goals and go all out for it with a strong drive. And I do like Atiku also because his wife, Titi, is from the South. Whenever I see Northerners who marry Southerners, or Easterners who marry Westerners, and seemingly live happily together, I loyally assume that they are "detribalised" Nigerians. That's the mental picture I had of Atiku. But when he started to apply his drive and tenacity to pushing the "zoning" thing, my loyalty began to question his loyalty. I reflected upon the term "absolute loyalty" and wondered that if a man is not absolutely loyal to the idea of "one nation bound in UNITY" and still plays the tribal card, or if a man is not absolutely loyal to his own political party – dumping the party and saying all sorts of things against it, when he couldn't clinch the ticket only to return when he needs that ticket, why should he get my vote? Would a man who was not "absolutely loyal" to the administration in which he served as vice-president be loyal to the nation if he should come into power as president? I dumped the thought. That's the business of his party, not mine. And by the way, such actions are not uncommon across the general political landscape so one might as well not take that against Atiku. Many such things are "normal" in Nigeria. I laughed.

My thoughts drifted again into state level politics in which several governors and their deputies are permanently polarised. And in many instances, the schism will be so obvious and yet the deputy governors will insist on sitting tight as part of the administration. You would see a governor having his own loyalists within the administration while his deputy has parallel loyalists. Yet it would be the same administration. The deputy would not resign. If he ever gets out of that administration, it would be by impeachment from the governor's loyalists. I muse to myself "absolute and non-absolute loyalties". The whole political scenery looks like some Neanderthal drama. I laughed again.

How long shall this sort of things continue in this country? A marriage of convenience is easily celebrated but it is also easily dissolved and often has debilitating effects on the children. Today, we are seeing a repetition of many such marriages again as the elections draw near. People who have sharply criticised one another are pairing together to form alliance just to win. If they win, their respective missions will already be accomplished at merely winning and their differences will play out when they are sworn in. Then the schism will start again. *No be laughing matter o.*

Chapter 4

We Too Dey Laugh O

Atiku to Obasanjo: 'We too dey laugh ooo!'
-       The Nation, 27 November 2010.

We Too Dey Laugh O

Earlier in this book, I mentioned the fact that we copied the American political system wrongly. It's not that the Americans do not do smear campaigns during their elections, in fact, they often do. However, they do it with more finesse than we apply.

Let me remind you. In the last week of November 2010, two newsworthy events occurred. Atiku had emerged as the consensus candidate amongst 4 major aspirants from the North. Then, Rauf Aregbesola had also been declared Governor of Osun state more than 43 months after the gubernatorial election. (Normally a governor is to serve for 48 months). Reporters sought Obasanjo's comments about Atiku's emergence as "consensus candidate". Obasanjo laughed. Then the campaign organisation of Atiku also laughed, but in its "laughter statement", the organisation also blamed Obasanjo for the woes of the PDP in the "entire Southwest" and the "entire nation", citing the fact that the PDP lost the case to Aregbesola at the appeals due to the way Obasanjo had handled the party. Hmmn. The organisation failed to see that when the people were voting, Atiku was Obasanjo's vice-president but was contesting on the platform of the ACN, Aregbesola's party. Could we then say it was Obasanjo rather than Atiku who worked against the PDP in Osun state in 2007?

You know what? When Atiku emerged as the consensus candidate, I felt that his chances of winning his ticket had become brighter than that of Jonathan. Atiku now represents 4 formidable aspirants and their respective supporters while Jonathan represents only himself and his supporters. I saw the possibility of Atiku becoming the flag-bearer of the PDP in the presidential election. But for the fact that the PDP had put the primaries so close to the INEC deadline for submission of nominated candidates, I felt that Atiku had made the President the underdog. If Atiku lost the primaries, and there was still time, he would have the option of running to another party as before but the President would be unable to run to another party. It would be "too indecorous" for a sitting president to leave his party and campaign under the flag of another party. However, when Atiku's campaign organisation laughed, I wondered if the laughter was politically correct. The campaign organisation made many negative comments about Obasanjo, who is the sitting Chairman of the Board of Trustees of the PDP. I wondered if the campaign organisation had concluded that Atiku could not win the party's ticket. Otherwise, if they expected Atiku to win, didn't they realise that the Chairman of their party's BOT would be on their campaign train if their candidate won?

Well, they have a right to laugh anyway. Possibly, there are no rules to laughing otherwise some laughter would not be right. It turned out afterwards, though, that Atiku lost and the time-table was done in such a way that even if he wanted to run to another party, there was no time to run. Now, I understand why his campaign team had laughed.

Teacher, Don't Teach Me Nonsense

If there were no rules, talking about right and wrong would only help to generate confusion. What can you make of this statement – "*The Left is right. The Right is wrong. The wrong are on the left*". Nonsense, isn't it? Well, not really. You see, where this idea of political parties and legislative systems originated they have a traditional seating arrangement in which the government and the opposition sit opposite each other and engage each other in debates over governmental policies. Those who favoured the traditional order were on the right side, those who favoured radical change were on the left. Eventually, the term settled in irrespective of the physical seating arrangement.

Where we copied this pattern on bi-cameral legislative system, there are basically two major political parties. One is known to support conservative religious and family values and free-market systems, the other supports social change and deregulation of several sectors of the economy. Each party has distinctive ideological characteristics. Here in Nigeria things are different.

Let me show you a bit of Nigerian politics and sociology:

Teacher:	Tell me, which Nigerian political party supports conservative religious and family values?
Student:	All of them.
Teacher:	Which Nigerian political party is pro-life?
Student:	All of them.
Teacher:	Which Nigerian political party is pro-abortion?
Student:	None of them.
Teacher:	Which Nigerian political party supports gun control?
Student:	All of them. In fact, they all support bomb control and kidnapping control.
Teacher:	Which Nigerian political party supports tax cuts?
Student:	None of them.
Teacher:	Which Nigerian political party supports resource control?
Student:	None is either for or against it.
Teacher:	So, why then are there so many different political parties?
Student:	Excuse me, Teacher, don't teach me nonsense. What's our business with gun control or tax cuts or pro-abortion or the separation of religion and state? That's not what we are talking about here. Is that what you call politics? We need potable water, good roads, regular electricity, free food, free clothes, free houses . . . free fathers, free mothers, free wives and free children. Government should share money. We don't need to work. The money is there. God has blessed our country with plenty of money. But some people are just *eating* the money. They don't allow it to go round.

You are talking of tax. Why should we pay tax? What about our oil money, have they finished sharing that one? Oh, oh . . . we should then go and *dash* them our tax again, after they have *eaten* all our oil money! See, Teacher, please go back to Britain or wherever you come from. Don't teach me nonsense. Who cares about taxes? *Lefti ko, righti ni.*

Do you understand better now? The bulk of the Nigerian people have a lot of unrealistic expectations, and the few who have money enough to promise us the moon ride on our fantasies. They would always promise us heaven and earth but won't give us as much as just a foothold.

> *Why can't all the other parties in Nigeria unite and form one large alternative to the ruling party? Selfishness. That's just the simple answer.*

Someone said to me "the Government is our problem". I told him, "no, it's the opposition. There's no formidable opposition to balance power with the Government and rather than unite to form a formidable opposition, every one pursues its own ambitions". It wasn't until very recently that I learnt that Nigeria has 63 registered political parties, 18 of which are seeking to present a presidential candidate. Rather than sit together, and compare their scripts – if they have any – and unite to form a sort of consensus party, not on the basis of where they come from or which aspirants they support but on the basis of their ideological characteristics, each party aligns according to the personal ambitions of its leaders.

There are, at present, 10 political parties and 1 independent represented in the United Kingdom House of Commons. Two parties form the Government while the remaining 8 form the opposition. The opposition is one team. The United States whose form of Government we copy has only 2 parties in the Congress. Why can't all the other parties in Nigeria unite and form one large alternative to the ruling party? Selfishness. That's just the simple answer. Yet they too laugh.

They laugh at the ruling party and make comments to incite laughter (ridicule) from the people against the government. Well, I think our miseries have become laughing matters. Or, haven't they?

The Evil Genius

Ibrahim Badamosi Babangida was until recently aspiring to return to Aso Rock. I like him. He's very intelligent. I always like intelligent people. But I don't always like it when someone believes that he or she is the only person that can fix all the problems faced by the country. Babangida was our military president for 8 straight years. He managed an economy in crisis and eventually was considered the cause of the crisis himself.

But having been there for 8 years, I wonder why he would need to come back. Does it mean that he believes there are no other intelligent persons in Nigeria?

When Babangida came into power in 1985, he gave the excuse that the Buhari regime perpetrated gross human rights abuses although himself had been a very senior member of the Buhari regime. The country was going through a period of chronic and severe austerity. More than 40% of the budget was being voted for debt servicing. Babangida listened to the IMF and World Bank and launched the Structural Adjustment Programme. Really, there wasn't much else he could do than comply with the recommendations of those bodies. Without the SAP, the country would have continued to engineer commodity prices at a continual loss and possibly we would have arrived at a point where possibly 90 to 100 % of the budget would have had to be earmarked for debt servicing.

Babangida was not just a military head of state; he was in fact a "president" because his style of governance was largely consultative. He is arguably one of the most dynamic and democratic of the military rulers we have had. However, the common man in the street knows that Babangida met the exchange rate at about 0.9 Naira per dollar but left it at about 21 Naira per dollar. We blame Babangida for devaluating the Naira. We blame Babangida for causing inflation. But we hardly see the fact that the idea of devaluing the Naira was originally that of the IMF and the World Bank and not Babangida's.

47

See, Babangida had cleverness and a sense of good governance. But the third element of what makes it all fuse together successfully was not always present – good luck. Babangida came into power in the midst of rising inflation and lowering oil prices. The Nigerian economy has been largely dependent on oil incomes. Oil prices were about $35 per barrel in 1980 in nominal price terms but in real price terms adjusting for inflation, that is like $93 today[9]. By 1986, oil prices had dropped to about $10 per barrel which is like $27 today. The common man on the streets does not understand what this means. It means that the country was much poorer under the first 5 years of Babangida that it used to be in the 70s and early 80s and of course in this century. Babangida originally stated that he would hand over power to civilians in 1990, but then 1990 brought an unexpected blessing. The pressure of oil prices had contributed to the collapse of the then USSR, which had become a major oil producer. The disintegration of the USSR as well as Iraq's invasion of Kuwait, which would later result in the Gulf War, among other factors, affected the global crude oil prices. The effects of these were a windfall of oil money on the Nigerian nation.

Babangida had cleverness and a sense of good governance. But the third element of what makes it all fuse together successfully was not always present – good luck.

Suddenly, the government had money to spend. And rather than just conduct an election and leave, it apparently just decided to wait and spend the money. Not entirely for corrupt reasons, perhaps. It was seemingly an opportunity for Babangida to transform himself into the ideal "messiah" for the country he must have imagined he would be when he took the reins in 1985. He postponed his exit from the Government but gave us a mix of both military and civilian administration. He had a vision of giving us detribalised political parties – and by his military decree, the only way you could enter

---

[9] See *Real and Nominal Oil Prices Since 1970* in the Wall Street Journal Online

into politics was either through the Left-leaning Social Democratic Party or the Right-leaning National Republican Party. It was a good concept. Whether the concept became realised is another argument.

Along the line, the 1990 coup, in which he was accused of running an "homosexually-centred" government and aiming at keeping himself in office for life seemingly forced him to hurry up the relocation of the seat of Government from Lagos to Abuja; forcing the government to spend more money on providing the necessary physical structures to run the government from Abuja while that could have been otherwise used to consolidate the economy.

Ultimately, his annulment of the 1993 presidential elections allegedly won by M. K. O. Abiola is possibly the most unfortunate decision of the Babangida regime. He finally "stepped aside" on August 27, 1993 and left power without pulling the nation out of the rubble, and the attendant crisis of a still-birth transition to civil administration.

So, you would ask, would I agree that Babangida should govern this country again? Would I vote for him if he runs for the office of the president? No, I won't vote for him but not for the common reasons. I won't vote for Babangida not because he annulled the June 12, 1993 election which was worn by a Yoruba man, who incidentally had also been his personal friend. I don't care about the tribe of the man who won the elections. I won't vote for Babangida not because he devalued the Naira – it was not his idea, it was the idea of the World Bank and the IMF. I won't vote for Babangida, not because he has failed to respond to calls for him to explain the death of Dele Giwa, or

> *I won't vote for Babangida not because he annulled the June 12, 1993 elections which was worn by a Yoruba man, who incidentally had also been his personal friend. I don't care about the tribe of the man who won the elections.*

how his administration managed the 1990 oil windfall which was estimated at over $12 billion. I just won't vote for him simply because I feel he had been the "president" long enough. After all, he had 8 years in power and ran a widely-consultative administration. Elected presidents are not supposed to be in office longer than 8 years by our constitution. When I look at the circumstances under which Babangida came into power, and the prevalent realities of his years in power, I don't think he would have performed any better than he did had he been an elected president.

I have never met Babangida. But if I have the opportunity of meeting him, I would tell him, "Your Excellency, sir, you have already done your best for this country. You really tried. A man cannot do more than his best. I don't think there is anything else you could do than you have done. That's not to mean that you have nothing more to offer, it simply means, I don't think you can do any better now than you did back then. Your style was democratic. So, I look at you as though you had been an elected president for 8 years. Why don't you just set up a foundation, possibly an NGO caring for victims of ethnic conflicts or bomb blasts, and widows and orphans of bomb blast victims and human rights abuses across Africa? Why don't you take on a larger role like setting up a Centre for Political Consensus Initiatives, where political parties can come together to negotiate ideologies and form detribalised mergers that would balance power with the government? You are after all a GCFR – Grand Commander of the Federal Republic – there's no higher honour you can aspire to in this country. So, hold your peace, sir, and don't always give in to the pressures on you to run for office of the president. If I were you, sir, it would seem to me that I had been president long enough. You already made your marks and they will ever be indelible. Take time and do "something Federal and National". Sir, can you see General Gowon? You see what he's doing with Nigeria Prays? Can you set up something like that? God bless you. Just kindly do some NGOs instead of trying to be president again. The country will like you more for that, and the legacies of that will be cherished long after you are dead". Honestly, that's what I would say.

Curse Not The King

I have often heard many people say things about leaders and political office holders in this country that I often take as mere "back of the class murmurings". You know what? As a rule, I do not say things behind a man that I will find impossible to repeat in his presence. It's a principle I learnt from the Bible –

> *Do not revile the king even in your thoughts,*
> *or curse the rich in your bedroom,*
> *because a bird of the air may carry your words,*
> *and a bird on the wing may report what you say.*
> (Ecclesiastes 10: 20)

See, before I blame the Government for anything, I always try to imagine what I could have done if I were in their shoes – that is if I had the same size of feet, though. I always try and ask myself that if I have had the same backgrounds, the same educational training and career history, the same connections and exposure, and the same opportunities as the man in power, would I make better decisions? And that's the question I ask when trying to decide who to vote for. I understand that the quality of decisions a man would make would be influenced by his personal history, education and exposure – not basically his ethnicity or religion.

Great Men Are Not Always Wise

At present, there is a team running for the office of the president and vice-president who have been known for their religious commitments, discipline and anti-corruption stance. While I am very excited about them, I am also cautioned that it takes more than religious piety to govern a nation.

Many of us, ordinary citizens, in the country think of a president as an individual. In real terms, a president is not just an individual. Often more than not, a president is just the voice of an institution. Presidents are extremely busy people and they always have

I am also cautioned that it takes more than religious piety to govern a nation.

51

more to do than can ever be done. In a single day, there will be more for the president to read than many of us actually read in an entire year. For conversations, if every of the 36 State Governors, or 40-something ministers, not counting the 109 Senators or the 360 Members of the House Representative have their respective wishes, each of them would like to have a 5-minute private dialogue with the president every week. Yet the president must attend public functions and meetings, and yet be a husband to his wife, and father to his children. There will be bills to read, understand and sign. There will be letters from various persons and organisations. There will be unscheduled and unplanned visits to disaster areas. And more importantly, there will be planning to do. I mean, serious planning and critical decision making amidst conflicting alternatives.

So, how do they manage to do the job? In most cases, it's not the president as a person that does most of the presidential jobs. It's often the aides – the chief of staff, special advisers, senior special assistants, special assistants and personal assistants. Most speeches read by most presidents are not in fact prepared by them. Obasanjo was said to often write his own speeches but I presume that cannot practically be every time. Even presidents of the developed countries often have dedicated speechwriters. So, when you hear a president making a brilliant speech – it's often the brilliance from the mind of another individual. Most letters are replied on behalf of a president. Most decisions are taken on behalf of a president. And where a president takes his own decisions, he would often have to rely on the wisdom and advice of several, if not many, people.

So, you are thinking of voting in one person who will turn the country around? Well, think again. The person that will turn the country around must be someone who knows how to do intensive academic and analytical thinking. He has to sift through myriads of opinions and advises at breakneck speed while trying not to spoil the team spirit among his aides. Some people can't even administer a committee of 6 people, and yet they will open their mouths loudly to say a particular president is not doing anything. Some people can't even make a success of being husband of one wife without problems, yet they will blame and curse a president.

52

Being president is not an easy task. You have to understand the complexity of administration in order to appreciate what presidents do. The basic job of the president is to wisely select and appoint his aides who would be his tentacles, doing his job in his name. However, the major problem with the selection and appointment of presidential aides is that often a president is not free enough to choose his own aides. There will be pressure from his political party. There will be pressure from friends and acquaintances. There will be pressures from his sponsors and those who worked assiduously to ensure he won the election. In our country, because those positions seemingly afford the occupiers some undue advantages, filling the posts becomes a means of rewarding those who worked to put you in the office. I have seen the pattern across various levels of Government – not just at the presidential level, and across political parties, without exception. I watched an interview on a state television channel in which a governor was questioned on why he didn't have several women as commissioners in his cabinet. He bluntly answered that there were people who worked for him to win the election in the first place and that he couldn't leave aside those people to appoint women as his commissioners. He rationalised that he would not have been governor in the first place if the men did not work for him to win the election. As a result, they deserved to be appointed as commissioners. How very interesting!

So, you think the "pious pair" will be different? Because of their anti-corruption stance and reputation for zero-tolerance to indiscipline? *I pray o.* What I know is that they will owe favours, and those favours will be paid with appointments and slots; and it is in fact those "appointments and slots" that do the bulk of the duties designated for a president and vice-president – they will write speeches; advise and

So, you are thinking of voting in one person who will turn the country around? Well, think again.

make decisions on behalf of, and in the name of, the president. They will in fact laugh on behalf of the president too. *Dem too dey laugh.*

To Serve Nigeria is Not By Force

In Nigeria, we have a way of laughing at our miseries. We have a lot of stand-up comedians, who have recently turned professional anyway, that make us laugh at stuff we should actually weep about. In a series tagged "night of a thousand laughs", the comedians will make jest of a lot of ugly situations in Nigeria and we would all laugh about it.

One comedian will talk about how Warri boys could forcefully threaten you and obtain your possessions from you in broad daylight, and yet we would laugh. Another will talk about how policemen will threaten you on the highway and ask you all sorts of questions just to make you part with N20 ($0.13) or N50 ($0.33) and yet we would laugh over it. Yet another comedian will talk about how the feeding formula has changed in many homes from 1-1-1 (breakfast-lunch-dinner) to 1-0-1 (breakfast-no-lunch-dinner), or 0-0-1 (no-breakfast-no-lunch-just-dinner), and we would laugh over it. Yet we all know that these are not actually supposed to be laughable issues, and even when the comedians jest at us that "we are suffering and smiling", we would yet laugh at that. *All of us dey laugh o. Abi?*

One particular jest caught my attention. In the words of our national anthem, there's the part that says "to serve Nigeria with all my strength". Some comedians made a remix of it as "to serve Nigeria is not by force". I laugh. But indeed, that's the truth. To serve Nigeria is not by force.

A lot of our politicians style themselves as "servant of the people", "chief servant", "chief service officer". They would tell us, they are just there to serve, not for personal gain. How so? Why then are they so desperate to serve?

When the word "servants" is used, my idea of it is that of "stewards" – I mean people who bring food and drinks from the kitchens to the tables. If you were seated at a dinner, and you see stewards struggling with one another and brawling about who would serve you, breaking bottles and using the broken glass to stab each other, just to earn a right to serve your table, wouldn't you be wary of their true intentions? Is there more to service than just to serve?

We see a lot of politicians who would fight tooth and nail over the right to serve the country and yet they would claim that their intentions are just to serve and serve only. How true indeed!

See; always be wary of the *desperados* - people who want to govern the country or a state at all costs. They do not have the intentions of serving. A man has sought to become president on the platform of his party but after losing the primaries decideD to run on the platform of another party; again, not winning on the platform of that second party, he returns to his party and fights vehemently to win, shouldn't we wonder if there is more to his aspirations than just to serve?

Another man may have always been the presidential candidate of his party and if his party insists that he would not be automatically made the presidential candidate of the party this time around but would have to go through a primary election, he would decamp to another party. This man who feared that he might not win his party's primary elections would like to win the presidency of the country? And just because he is asked to go through a primary election, he quits the party that has featured him as the candidate 2 times, over an eight-year period? Is there more to his aspirations than just to serve? Indeed, to serve Nigeria is not by force.

> *See, always be wary of the desperados - people who wants to govern the country or a state at all costs.*

You, see, friend, all I have said in this book so far are preambles. Now, from the next chapter, I will say what I really want to say.

PART II

Endemic Problems of the Nigerian Society

Chapter 5

You, What Are You Doing?

"Ask not what your country can do for you; ask what you can do for your country"
John F. Kennedy, 35th President of the United States of America
20 January 1961

That first major accident.

Brace yourself. I am going to tell you a poignant story.

On Saturday, 24th March 2001, I was travelling to Lagos from Akure. I had joined my friend, Ade, and his family in their Peugeot 505 Salon car. Four of us sat at the back of the car. As we approached Ijebu Ode, it occurred to me to fasten the seat belt but I ignored it. I did so because I didn't want to be selfish. The back seat had 3 safety belts, but we were 4 at the back. Not too long after, the rear tyre at my side burst. I sat by the rear door on the right side. The vehicle had been going at a speed of about 120 kilometres per hour. In a jiffy, the car skidded off the road and rolled over. I hit my face against what only God knows. I must then have blacked out. Next, I heard Ade calling my name, and urging me *"Tope, let us get out of the car. The car is about to explode"*. I think the word *"explode"* further jolted me into consciousness. I realised then that the car was upside down. But I wasn't fully in control of myself. My feeble efforts to crawl out the car were in vain.

Some good Samaritans pulled me out. I was bleeding profusely from my mouth and nostrils. My shirt had to be thrown away because it was soaked in blood. The strangers that had stopped to help us rushed us to the General Hospital at Ijebu Ode. I was received at the Accidents and Emergency unit and placed on a metal stretcher. I was still bleeding. Ade feared that I might die. He had only a slight bruise on his head. I couldn't speak. I only managed to squeeze his hand. Just to reassure him that I still had my consciousness.

The nurses were good. They tried to clean the blood off me. Then, they discovered blood kept flowing from my nostrils. They immediately asked that I should rather be taken to the Ogun State University Teaching Hospital (OSUTH), as it was then called, at Sagamu. Why? There were no functional suction machines at General Hospital Ijebu-Ode to clear the blood they feared was filling my lungs.

We got to Sagamu and I was put in the emergency ward. Minutes later, nurses attached a drip set to my right hand for intravenous infusions. I found the mattress comfortable and rolled on my sides a little bit. After all, at Ijebu Ode I had been put on only a metal stretcher with no soft covering at all. And I had arrived at OSUTH squeezed up on the back seat of a salon car.

Then, the nurses surprised me. They were not comfortable that I was rolling on my sides on the bed. They brought out long bandages and tied my left hand and my legs to the edges of the bed. I protested but they ignored my protests. When they left me, I crossed my right arm over to free my left arm and managed to sit up and free my legs. Then they began to *yab* me – *"You are stubborn, if you fall down from that bed no one will carry you up o"*. I told them *"I won't fall down, I'm conscious"*. One of them gently explained to me that there's a massive head injury and that patients with head injuries often present unpredictable behaviours and as a precaution they were tying me to the bed with bandages. I told her, *"I know what I am doing and won't fall off the bed"*. They left me. Good. I had some peace. But blood was still flowing from my nostrils.

I overheard the nurses discussing between themselves that I had lost so much blood and possibly would need some transfusion. They sent for the doctor on call. I overheard them discussing that someone should go and check if the haematology laboratory was open, so they could do a test for my blood group. I told them what my blood group is but they ignored me.

Then I must have slept off or something. The next thing I realised was that Ade came to wake me and asked, *"How much do you have on you?"*. *"I'm not really sure"*, I answered, *"the cash on me is in my inner pocket"*. Then he told me *"They said we would need about 10,000 Naira for ambulance. They are thinking of transferring you to the UCH"*. UCH is the University College Hospital at Ibadan.

That would be like a 2-hour journey. I asked him *"Why?"*. He answered, *"They said their ENT doctors would not be available until Monday and the blood from your nose is still flowing. They fear you might not make it through the night."* I told him, *"don't worry. I would not die. I would make it through the night"*. He said, *"If you see yourself, you won't speak this way"*. Then, he left and said he would be back. I guess it was just because we did not have 10,000 Naira to hire the ambulance from the OSUTH that I was not transferred to UCH that night.

I had my mouth opened throughout the night. I was breathing through the mouth. The two nostrils were blocked. When I woke up in the morning, I closed my mouth and found that some air could flow through one of my nostrils. A nurse came to check me. She said, *"Congratulations. The blood that was flowing from your nostrils has stopped. Please don't touch your nose. If you touch the nose, the bleeding might resume and you will just die away"*. (She spoke in Yoruba). I marvelled at the crudeness of her kindness. The words *"you will just die away"* re-echoed in my head.

When she left, I thought to myself, *"If air could manage to come through this nostril and blood is not coming through, I can try to clear the clots."* And so with my bare fingers, I began to remove blood clots from that nostril. It became free enough for me to breathe comfortably without the other nostril. I reassured myself, *"I shall not die but live to declare the glory of God"*.

I was kept on intravenous infusion throughout Sunday. Then Monday morning, the drip set was removed and I was served a bowl of pap and given a boiled egg. I sat up and took the pap. Then I discovered I was in big trouble. I tried to eat the boiled egg but found I could not bite it. Rather than cut into the egg, a whole block of the teeth in my mouth seemed to be too weak to bite the egg. I put the egg

So, rather than being informed by the hospital that I had a fracture, it turned out the other way round. And that was a teaching hospital – a tertiary health institution.

back into the plate and put two fingers into my mouth. I found that the right ride of my upper palate was movable from side to side on its own. I said to myself, "*this is serious*". I informed the nurse that I couldn't bite the egg and related what I had just discovered – a fracture in my upper palate. It was nearly 2 full days after the accident and no X-rays had been taken. So, rather than being informed by the hospital that I had a fracture, it turned out the other way round. And that was a teaching hospital – a tertiary health institution.

> *. . . at least three elements must combine to bring about the positive change we all desire to witness in this country. The three elements are cleverness, good governance and good luck.*

Who says luck does not exist? I was lucky to have survived! Weeks later, when I was operated upon at the Obafemi Awolowo University Teaching Hospital Ile-Ife to correct the displacement of my right zygoma bone, the doctor explained to me that the brain sits partly at an angle above the nasal bone and that if the force that fractured my maxilla and caused a displacement of the zygoma had directly impacted my nasal none, it could have pushed that bone upwards into the brain and may have been fatal. "You are lucky to have survived", he told me. I knew.

Cleverness, Good Governance and Good Luck

You must wonder why I am telling you all this and then linking it up to the word "luck". So as to make you vote for any particular candidate? NO. And that's a capital 'N' and 'O'. I said it earlier that my personal convictions mean that I must be "politically neutral" in public. As much as possible, I will try and do that in this little book. Yet while being "neutral", I will try as much as possible to point out to you that at least three elements must combine to bring about the positive change we all desire to witness in this country. The three elements are cleverness, good governance and good luck.

See, the idea is not mine. I have only paraphrased a parallel reasoning. One of these days I was watching a programme on the National Geographic channel. The narrator was describing a battle between predators in the wild. It was a battle fuelled by the survival and basic instincts of each of the species rather than animosity, jealousy and greed as we often see in the animal called man. The narrator said, "*As in any battle, the outcome is determined by strategy, skill and a little luck*". And it's from this that I cloned "cleverness [for strategy], good governance [for skill], and good luck [for a little luck]".

Those who are very close to me know very well that I am not the type that will say things like "*this is who to vote for, don't vote for that*". You probably didn't read my first book, *Does God Truly Exist?* , or else you wouldn't think I am campaigning for someone in particular. In any argument that involves urging people to make a choice, my particular style is to demonstrate to you the merits and demerits of the different options and then urge you to "make a wise choice". *Does God Truly Exist?* is written in 3 parts. The third and final part has the caption "make a wise choice". Similarly, in this present book, my final chapter is captioned, "I Wish You Only the Best". That is, whoever you think the best of the candidates might be. However, I must show you how cleverness influences good governance, how good governance influences good luck, and how good luck can make you cleverer. It's a cycle of life.

You, What Are You Doing?

After the accident I described above, I had a surgery at the Obafemi Awolowo University Teaching Hospital, Ile-Ife, in April 2001. Then my jaws were immobilised in what is called IMF (Intermaxillary Fixation). A strong metal arc was used to brace my entire lower teeth and another was done for the upper teeth, and then both were tied together with smaller strings of metals. I lived on only water, juices, custards and milk for the next 8 weeks. It was a trying time but I was so glad and grateful to have survived.

I think, sometime around July that year, I was visiting Ibadan. Before the accident, I usually travelled to Ibadan almost every weekend. (I will tell you why later in this chapter). I resumed the practice just as soon as I was free from the treatments.

There's a popular store at Bodija called Favos. It's on a street that forms a T-junction with the Secretariat-UI road. I had gone to browse at a cafe in the Favos building. Then I crossed to the side of the road and walked towards Awolowo Junction – the road connecting to Sango.

As I crossed Awolowo Junction, I noticed a police van. There was a police man walking away from the van towards the centre of the junction. He was raising his rifle and it happened to be pointing in my direction. I was scared. Because I have always heard one story or another of "accidental discharge" of police bullets, I decided to avoid being in direct line of the rifle. Just in case anything went wrong accidentally. (*Olorun maje a ri Esu*).

I crossed the junction and waited past the van. There was another young man waiting on my left between the van and me. There were several other people on my right too. I was waiting to catch a bus or cab, and must presume that's what other people were waiting for at that junction too. The time would have been about 8 pm.

Suddenly, I heard a gunshot. The police man who was raising his rifle fired into the air. I was jolted. I didn't see why he had to shoot into the air. There were no riots. Everything was normal and going on fine. I looked in his direction. I saw him hanging the rifle on his shoulders and walking towards us. He accosted the man who stood to my left, closest to the van, and asked him *"You, what are you doing?"*. (He spoke in Yoruba). The man responded, *"I'm waiting for a vehicle"*. He gave the man a resounding slap – and yelled at him *"Is that what you do for a living?"* The young man responded in disbelief, *"Ah ah, your question could be ambiguous – I thought you were asking about what I am doing on this spot"*. The policeman slapped him again, *"Is that what you do for a living?"*. Every other person waiting for bus or cab quickly moved further away from the scene. That was shocking. I mean, crazy.

From a reasonable distance I watched as the young man told him *"I'm a student"*. The policeman retorted, *"You are a student? Where's your ID card?"* Unfortunately, the young man fumbled him pockets but couldn't produce an ID card. He was bundled into the back of the police van. Ever since I witnessed that event, I have never gone out of my house again without an ID card.

That's our country. That's part of the good effort the police make to protect us. *Na so, now.*

I was lucky I wasn't the one standing closest to the police van. It could have been me. My wounded mouth that had only managed to heal up would have been smashed by those terrible slaps. That policeman had such a bulky frame; I bet I would have fainted if I had been the one he slapped.

Cleverness Can Make You Lucky

Luck is complex and may be hard to understand. How then would I explain here without unnecessarily bothering you? See, most Nigerians grow up dreading the subjects of Mathematics and English Language in elementary school. Results show that many students often fail in these subjects and keep re-sitting school leaving certificate examinations just because of these subjects. Yet the subjects form the key to understanding other subjects through which we are instructed on how life around us is generally organised and governed.

In Mathematics, there are the terms "combination" and "permutation". For example, you can keep sensitive documents or cash in a safe. Usually, a safe has a combination lock. You will be required to lock and unlock the safe with a set of numbers, say 456. In Mathematics, that's actually called "permutation" because the combination must follow a certain order. If you used 564 instead of 456, the lock will simply not open. It doesn't matter that you have a combination of a "4", a "5", and a "6"; in as much as it doesn't combine in the exact order in which it should, it wouldn't work. In real life, luck could be expressed as a permutation resulting from an accidental combination. We are not all mathematicians, so I will spare you the labours of thinking through that.

However, I will show you the importance of the word "IF" as it relates to luck. You see, the day I had that accident, Mama had travelled to the village. When she was leaving, she had invited me to join her on her trip. I declined. Mama counselled that since I was not travelling with her to the village, I should wait at Akure and not go with Ade to Lagos. Ade had just graduated from the University. She was aware that Ade's dad was coming from Lagos that day to pick him and his baggage. After Mama embarked on her journey, I still joined

Ade and his family for the journey to Lagos, stubbornly ignoring Mama's counsel.

When we were setting out of Akure, Ade's dad commented to the driver – "*can you see that the tyre we feared would give us problem did not give us any problem at all, all the way from Badagry to Akure. God who saw us through from Badagry to Akure will see us through the return journey*". We all said, "*Amen*". And of course, God did see us through, except for the fact that the bad tyre burst before we could get to Ijebu Ode and the vehicle somersaulted and I fractured my upper jaw. What IF I had listened to Mama and had not joined Ade and his family for that trip, what IF Ade's dad had replaced his vehicle's bad tyre, would I have been in an accident that day? I don't think so. The accident was due to negligence. Someone didn't replace the bad tyre but rather preferred to trust God to take care of it. (Not that I blame him, it wasn't his best wishes not to change the bad tyre. It was economic considerations that had forced him to keep "managing" the worn out tyre). You see why I said earlier that if we Nigerians have our way, we would rather defecate and trust God to pack our faeces. The moral of it all is this, when you make bad choices, like deciding to travel with a bad tyre, you are prone to running into bad luck.

Conversely, when you make good choices, like being clever enough to give a wide berth to a "trigger-happy" policeman, it could save you from dirty slaps.

These are trivial examples. The more important and present considerations are the choices we would be making during the coming elections. Some of us, no doubt, will not be clever enough to vote right. Some of us would still vote for a man who never really cared about us, just because he comes from the same ethnic background as we do. We would hope that God will save us from the dangers of a "bad-tyre" politician. God won't. We would bear the brunt eventually, if we leave aside the right choices and choose the wrong persons.

While voting for the wrong persons is bad, abstaining from voting is worse. Of course, if I am writing this, you should know it's not targeted at the illiterate,or semi-illiterate, voter. I am not targeting the bus-station tout, or the palm-wine-seller. Don't get me wrong, those people vote and their votes count big time. But in most cases they vote wrongly. They have no insight into macroeconomics and how it interplays with their daily lives. So, they simply make choices based on puerile factors – like the ethnicity of the candidate, or his eloquence and oratorical skills, or simply how flamboyantly he is dressed. That's probably why you see the politicians wearing so many fanciful clothes to the campaign rallies. Their dressing has a way of impressing the illiterate or semi-illiterate voters and the politicians seemingly have a way of capitalising on that.

Rather than target the illiterate and semi-illiterate voters, I am writing this for the literate persons because it is often the literate ones who abstain from voting. The literate person is relatively comfortable in the society, at present. He has a fairly good job. He lives in a big town or city. When the PHCN cuts power, which could be up to 4 times daily or whole days and whole weekends without a minute of power supply at all, the literate person has a standby generator. He has a concrete-ringed well, or borehole, and pumps water into an overhead storage tank for his family. He has one or two serviceable cars, and can still afford to fuel them regularly. For cash supply, he easily gets "no-wahala" loan from his bank. So, he is not really bothered whether it is candidate A or B that wins the election. Therefore, he does not vote or involve himself in the voting process. That's not clever.

See, our country enjoyed oil boom in the 70's and early 80s. The world was going through an energy crisis. Prices of oil skyrocketed. Oil producing countries made money. One of our Heads of State back then reportedly said, *"The problem with Nigeria is not the availability of money, but how to spend it"*. (I will return to this later). But suddenly, the bubble burst. A glut in the international oil market forced a collapse in the prices of crude oil. Our government had to recourse to austerity

We would hope that God will save us from the dangers of a "bad-tyre" politician. God won't. We would bear the brunt eventually, if we leave aside the right choices and choose the wrong persons.

measures. It could happen again! I mean, it could really happen again.

That is why as a literate person you have to take part in this year's election exercise. Don't feel secure enough with your economic situation and social status as to leave the voting in the hands of those who will only vote in "bad-tyre" politicians. I understand that, like I used to be, you may fear losing your limbs in the process. Yet I think there are effective steps you can take to ensure your personal safety during the elections and there are pre-electoral moves you can make like *"putting your mouth where your vote goes"* that I shall discuss in this book.

I have met many people who said that they only registered as voters just so as to have voters' card in case their employers would insist on not paying salaries to anyone who doesn't have a voter's card. Voting, I believe is a voluntary thing. One should not be compelled to vote. Indeed, there are employers – especially state governors, and heads of government agencies, who threaten their employees over not registering as voters. I do not agree that people must be coerced to vote.

Your decision to vote and put your mouth where your vote goes can make our country lucky.

What has luck got to do with it?
You might want to ask, what has luck got to do with it? I would say: everything. Let me ask you, is there any guarantee you will be alive in the next 10 years or 10 days? The fact that you are alive today, not sick, not on any target list by any assassin, or whatever, does not guarantee your continuous living. People die daily not by their own making. This is a painful example. On September 11, 2001, many people, successful professionals in their respective careers, left their homes in the morning and went to work as usual. Thousands of them died. They were not sick. They were not particularly on any assassin's hit list. They didn't think of it. They were not planning for it. But suddenly death came and took them. Because some other people elsewhere had a different plan.

I will give you yet another example. One of my favourite programmes on the National Geographic Wild channel is the "Caught in the Act", a programme that features videos recording of surprising and sometimes strange animal behaviours in the wild. In one episode, a leopard had caught a warthog and was struggling to bring it down, the warthog had kept whining. Her cries attracted yet another predator – a hyena. The hyena came and attacked the leopard. The warthog, at first, was surprised. It watched the predators for a short while and escaped into the bush. Obviously, given the level of animal intelligence, the hyena had not come with an intention to rescue the warthog. It probably had also wanted to come and kill the warthog for food. The warthog could not have been calling out to a hyena for rescue. It only happened that her cries of distress and danger attracted yet another enemy; but, ironically, when the danger increased, (because she was now amidst two predators), she escaped. That "happened" factor is called "luck".

It could be good or bad. But it interplays with everything we do in life. Sometimes you would have done everything you could to be successful at one thing and yet it fails, just because someone else "happened" to have done or not done something else. That is luck.

Cast your mind back. In 1983, there was a civilian administration. Then there were conflicts arising from the electoral process. Without the country voting for Buhari, he came on board. We didn't opt to be governed by the military. It just "happened" that because they found a crack in the wall, they came in. Then came also Babangida, not by the making of the country. And after the brief interim administration of Shonekan, we had Abacha. Then Abacha died in office and Abdulsalami Abubakar became the Head of State.

Come back, Abdulsalami Abubakar? Yes. But he was a Major General and there was a superior military officer – Jeremiah Useni – who was a Lieutenant General. Yes, but Abubakar was politically senior to Useni. You

Sometimes you would have done everything you could to be successful at one thing and yet it fails, just because someone else "happened" to have done or not done something else. That is luck.

see, when you are the Chief of Defence Staff, (that's the equivalent of the Chairman of the Joint Chiefs of Staff in the US) it means you are professionally the head of the armed forces. General Sani Abacha had kept the then Major General Abdulsalami Abubakar as CDS while keeping Lieutenant General Jeremiah Useni as Minister of the Federal Capital Territory. Thus, the Abdulsalami was a "boss" to his superior officer and that "luck" (with some other factors) made him Head of State instead of Useni when Abacha died.

The government records say autopsy reports confirmed Abacha's death as due to "natural causes"[10]. Useni says he was surprised because he had left Abacha as late as 2.30 am that night and was told that Abacha died at about 5 am. In a newspaper interview, he stated that many other people junior to him in rank had been informed and invited to the presidential villa after Abacha's death before he was invited. He attributes this to the possible fact that he was then being suspected of involvement in the cause of Abacha's death until the autopsy reports cleared him.

Replay. Pause at Abdusalami Abubakar. If things had been the way they ought to be from the beginning, he wouldn't have been Chief of Defence Staff while there was an officer senior in rank to him in the armed forces. It was his luck that he was the CDS when Abacha died.

No, you didn't get the full picture. It wasn't that Abacha didn't like to do things right. Back then there was another political office for military officers that was higher than the Chief of Defence Staff. That was Chief of General Staff. But the previous year, the Chief of General Staff, Lieutenant General Oladipo Diya had been arrested on allegations of plotting a coup against Abacha and had been tried by a military tribunal. The office of the Chief of General Staff was therefore vacant. Abacha, was probably wary of appointing the other Lieutenant General, Jeremiah Useni, as Chief of General Staff. So, here was luck. If there had been a Chief of General Staff, a Chief of Defence Staff would not have become Head of State when Abacha died. But even at that, Abubakar seems to have been "lucky" that he enjoyed the confidence of certain people who did not invite Useni into the presidential villa after Abacha died but rather chose to

---

[10] Washington Post, July 8, 1998

invite Abubakar. Poured into a glass, that episode still looks very cloudy to me, but I wouldn't like to pursue that now for here we're talking about luck.

Abubakar came in and promised to hand over to a democratically elected president within the next one year, and he did; unbelievably. When he made the promise, the country did not believe. We were expecting he would play the "Maradona game". Here was how one man's luck was again affecting the luck of the entire country.

Luck plays a significant role in everything. I mean, it plays a role even in your reading the present book. Why? Because the inspiration to write this book came to me as I reflected on the name of the incumbent president – Goodluck Jonathan. And I thought to myself, why not write a book titled *"Fellow Nigerians, I Wish You Good Luck"*. It would sound natural. After all, we always wish people good luck. It would have been different if the president has a different name. I won't be able to say *"I wish you Barack"*, for instance, or *"I wish you David"*, or *"I wish you Ibrahim"*, or *"I wish you Atiku"* because those are properly the names of specific individuals. But luckily, the president has a name that is close enough to the idea that I want to convey "good luck" as in "good fortune". "I wish you good luck", and here, though not as in the personal name of Mr. President which is spelt "Goodluck". So, relax. This is not a campaign.

> Luck plays a significant role in everything.

Good Luck Spreads

I am Yoruba. There is a Yoruba adage which translates as "if one man gets lucky, he makes 200 others lucky". I have already shown how the individual luck of our various heads of states over the years has affected the country. I don't need to belabour that argument.

I always like to read Abimbola Adelakun's column in the Punch. She's intelligent and witty. However, when she wrote "Goodluckism as a political philosophy" on 9th December 2010, I had to lean back and think carefully what about "good luck" means. I will extract two paragraphs from her writings here:

After listening to the advert for the umpteenth time, I asked myself, 'Do I really want good luck, as this advert has assumed on my behalf?' My answer is a vehement No!

It is not my place to tell his campaign team to thrash that good luck centered advert and recruit technocrats and thinkers who can put salubrious ideas together. Trying to use good luck as sentiment is cheap and shows a grave lack of depth. Even though we are a largely superstitious people, I believe we have had enough of good luck. Now is the time to start working hard, start planning ahead and run on merit.

In the first place, I guess she had muddled up what good luck means. To me, good luck is that inexplicable part that makes every right thing fall in place at the right time. When you have done all the best you could, it is very likely you will get the best result, but then there are no guarantees. Anything could still go wrong without your making and without a premonition. So, however in control of the situation I may find myself, I always pray for good luck. To say you have it all and don't need any more good luck is to underestimate the possibility of the interference of other persons and the acts of nature (or "acts of God", as it is in legal language) in your own plans.

> *good luck is that inexplicable part that makes every right thing fall in place at the right time.*

Yes, indeed, I wouldn't also like the idea of anything being sold to me on the basis of good luck alone. Yet, if anything works out fine, then it is good luck because it could always have been otherwise.

Remember, as I said earlier, three elements must combine for success – strategy, skill, and luck. However, luck is the link that connects everything. See, I can't but refer to the Holy Bible when I write or speak. It's authoritative and inspiring. And here's something the Bible says about luck:

Here is something else I have learned: The fastest runners and the greatest heroes don't always win races and battles. Wisdom, intelligence, and skill

*don't always make you healthy, rich, or popular. We each have our share of
bad luck.*

(Ecclesiastes 9: 11, Contemporary English Version)

The authorship of the verse I just quoted is attributed to Solomon, who has the
reputation of excellent wisdom. The moral of it is that, if you have what it takes
to succeed, and then you succeed, it means you have been lucky. If on the other
hand, you have what it takes to succeed, but in spite of everything that would
have ordinarily made you succeed, you do not succeed, then you have been
unlucky. That's what luck is.

In the example that I gave earlier about the policeman who slapped the young
man at the Awolowo junction. Tell me, what could the young man have done
otherwise? He was asked, *"You, what are you doing?"* And he innocently
answered, *"I'm waiting for a bus"*. And he got slapped for that. That was some
bad luck. Possibly that cop was drunk or something. Under different
circumstances, the same scenario could have played out with a different
outcome.

Harbingers of Luck
Years back, I had these friends who shared the stories of their secondary school
days. They were students at the Federal Government College, Odogbolu.
There were about four of them. Friends. They were boarding school students
and were required to get an exeat whenever they had to go out from the campus
during school term. The other way out was to sneak out illegally from the school
by finding some escape route to climb the fence into the city. Most times they
would sneak out of the campus and sneak back in, unnoticed. However, there
were times they got caught. Surprisingly, they realised that they always got
caught whenever one particular friend of theirs, Fischer*, joined them to sneak
out. For some inexplicable reasons, it just always happened to them that the
only times they got caught were the only times that Fischer joined them. They
made it a saying that *"Fischer na bad luck"*.

Friends, I don't know why there are stuff like that in life. I have read of a man
who said he married his wife for good luck. He had a small shop. The lady was
just a regular customer in his shop. Over a period of time, he noticed that any

73

day that a particular lady came to buy things from him; he would make so many sales that day. It looked like mere coincidence but it always worked for him. It got him curious about the lady and that was how their relationship started and led to a marriage.

If you look around, you will see one or two examples of such in life. I don't understand why. But it does happen. Good luck. Bad luck. Luck. It comes in various shapes and sizes. There are people that always get favoured in everything they do. There are others who hardly get favoured. The truth is that luck comes to each and every one of us. Yet it would seem that some are often "lucky", more than averagely, while some are often "unlucky" more than averagely. It happens.

I wouldn't tell you "go out and vote for Goodluck Jonathan", or for any other candidate for that matter. However, I think he is an easy example of the kind of "lucky" people I have used as examples. His political history shows a pattern of being in the favourable places at the favourable times. And what's more? He had been named "Goodluck" long before all these things started to play out in the eye of the public. Could there be more to it than mere luck? Could there be more to it than mere coincidence? A canoe-maker gave birth to a son and named him "Goodluck" and from that humble beginning Goodluck rose through many lucky instances to become the president of this country. Was he destined to be lucky? Why did his father name him Goodluck? Why not Joseph, or James, or Peter? They are questions I ponder about and smile to myself. And I must add that I ponder about them not for political reasons.

See, I have seen too much of coincidences in life. I lost my maternal uncle in a rollover accident on 27th May 2006. The rear tyre of the vehicle in which he was travelling came off. The vehicle rolled over. He died. Two of my aunts also passed on in that accident. It's to the three of them that I dedicated my book, *Does God Truly Exist?* Curiously, on 27th May 2008, I was also in a rollover accident. The rear tyre of the vehicle in which I was travelling came off. The coincidence of the dates and pattern of accidents still baffles me till today. Moreover, Uncle was Grandma's lastborn. I'm Mama's last born.

When Uncle died, we were told that he didn't die immediately the vehicle crashed. He had a bad head injury, we were told. Some sympathisers had met him still breathing in the carcass of the car but felt he was too wounded to make it. The two women had passed on immediately the car crashed. Of the survivors, he was the only one left un-rescued. One of the survivors in the crash, who was taken to the hospital, told me that it was over an hour after they were taken to the hospital that another set of sympathisers brought Uncle in. He was still breathing. He had been left to bleed for more than one full hour in the Sagamu-Ore expressway accident because the first set of rescuers felt he was too wounded to survive.

I am writing these things in pain and bewilderment. I'm bewildered because when I had the second major road accident on 27th May 2008, exactly 2 years after Uncle died, I was also at first neglected by rescuers. It was an 18-seat bus. Fully occupied. When the bus rolled over, something or someone – I don't know which – fell on my right arm; itt got broken. I realised it was broken when I tried to crawl out of the bus and tried to lift the arm but I couldn't control it. I crawled out with only my left arm. I was surprised when my right arm pulled along with me as I was pulling out of the bus. *"Oh,"* I thought to myself, *"it's not completely cut off"*. I sat by the roadside and saw sympathisers rushing other victims away, presumably to the hospital. No one was attending to me. I feared I would be left to die. History was replaying itself. I shouted *"Someone please help me, I'm bleeding to death!"*. I kept shouting. Some people answered from behind me, *"you are not bleeding too seriously, we are assisting people who are more wounded than you are"*. I didn't see their faces. I shouted, *"See, my arm is broken. I need you to get me to the hospital before pain sets in and kill me!"* For several minutes I was neglected. I prayed.

At last, I was helped to the hospital. Surprisingly, when we got to the hospital at Ilara-Mokin, which was not too far from the scene of the accident there were no doctors. There were just about 3 or 4 nurses; they were overwhelmed by the number of injured victims. Again I was neglected. I kept shouting, *"someone, please attend to me"*. A nurse shouted back that, *"Mr. Man, you have to be patient. We are suturing wounds of people who are more wounded than you are"*. I thought to myself, *"Oh my God"*.

Looking back today, I am grateful to have survived that accident. But I remain puzzled about coincidences. I would bore you if I begin to give you a catalogue of events in which coincidences play out in a significant way. But I will stop at this.

Coincidences and luck in the profile of our incumbent president has been a fascinating story. Unlike Abimbola, who wrote that she doesn't want good luck, I want good luck, though not necessarily from Mr. President. However, if I find myself locked up in a place, say like those four guys back then at Federal Government College, Odogbolu, and I need to get out of there by any means, I would rather choose to escape along with Goodluck than with Fischer. Fischer has a history of unfortunate recurrences, Goodluck has a history of fortunate uplifting. It is always better to travel in the company of someone who is an harbinger of good luck.

We can make our country lucky

If there's anyone who has suffered one or two disadvantages once too often just for being Nigerian, I can identify with such a person. I can list a number of opportunities I have lost just because Nigeria has earned a bad reputation in some circles. I trade on the internet and internationally. Nigeria has earned an unfortunate reputation of fraud, especially internet fraud, to a very unfair extent. Once I did search for the term "Nigeria" on the website of an international Christian booksellers association, the search returned 14 results. Each of the 14 results contained the word **fraud** boldly written. I was shocked. I changed the keyword to fraud, instead. Surprisingly, the search returned the same 14 results with each containing the name Nigeria. I was rather angry. They had made the words "fraud" and "Nigeria" synonymous, perhaps unintentionally. That factor, though, has affected many things we do here.

> *It is always better to travel in the company of someone who is a harbinger of good luck.*

There are companies that restrict business relationship with Nigeria just because we have been given a bad name, mostly unjustified. I could say that the country has made us unlucky, in a sense. However, I should delight to follow the injunction given by John F. Kennedy to his nation at his inauguration as the 35th President of the United States: "Ask not what your country can do for you; ask what you can do for your country" and with that, I won't mind the many opportunities I may have lost due to being Nigerian. I would rather seek to do my little bit to make this country great, and greater.

When I sit down and consider many opportunities that are open to us in this country, one thing I consider most important at this time is for us to reorganise the way the country is being run. By "being run", I am not referring to the roles of leaders alone; I am also referring to the roles of followers.

The greatest service I can do for my country today, as I write this book, is to tell you "vote wisely, vote right, and put your mouth where your vote goes". That's just one thing we can do to make our country lucky. If there is any among the candidates who is clever, if there is any among the candidates who has a record of good governance, and also has a record of being a harbinger of luck – on the good side – I would think voting for such a man would be one way to make the country lucky. We cannot rule out good luck in this matter, because in terms of what it takes to be a successful nation, we have it all, but it has never really worked. We need good luck to make it work. That's my take. The rest of my arguments are the post-climax.

Chapter 6

Golden Bombs and Misdirected Rockets

Nigeria independence celebrations marred by blasts
- BBC News Africa, 1st October 2010.

It's Crazy. No, It's a Shame

In the preface to this book, I had mentioned how my American friends would say, "it's crazy" and how that word is apparently ambiguous in its American use. One other word I picked from my foreign friends is "shame". I noticed it from the Brits. Here in Nigeria, you express your politeness or apology or regrets over a matter by saying "sorry" – even when you don't mean it. My British friends and cousins would rather say "it's a shame". As in, for instance, "it's a shame I couldn't help you when you needed a hand yesterday".

When in 2007, Ghana – Africa's first independent country had her golden anniversary, I thought of it that in just three years from then Nigeria's independence from Britain would also be 50 years old. I thought my country should plan ahead and prepare for the golden anniversary. It's a shame we are not built that way. We don't plan for anything until it is right upon us.

Let me give you a deeper insight. If Nigerians were invited to a wedding that would start at 10.00am, most of us would set out from our doors at 10.00am or a few minutes thereafter. So, we always end up being late. Always, I mean. We call it "African time". I am not sure other Africans take time for granted as much as we do, so I would rather suggest we start calling it "Nigerian time". Alas, that slothfulness earned us an international disgrace at our golden moment on the 1st of October, 2010.

While all eyes on this planet were on us, while the whole world watched to see how we would manage to crown the shoddy and last-minute preparations we had put together to mark our 50th anniversary, suddenly the news changed from celebrations to calamities. I have called them "shoddy" and "last minute" because, if this were not Nigeria, one would normally expect that the preparations for the celebrations would have been finalised at least since the previous year and the celebrations would have begun from 1st of January 2010 with a grand finale on 1st October 2010, for much less than the costs.

Alas on our "Golden Day", bombs exploded within a very short distance from the Eagles Square venue of the celebrations. There were at Eagles Square several heads of state and governments, or their representatives, from various parts of the world. Not just the Eagle Square but the entire Federal Capital Territory should have been on the highest security alert level for that period. It's a shame that the bombs were successfully planted and detonated.

I noted afterwards from the breakdown of the 9.5 Billion Naira budget for the anniversary celebrations that security had a vote of 500 million Naira; and I wondered why, in spite of this amount, we still failed to prevent the "golden bombs". Now, 500 million Naira is not a pretty big sum – it's about three and half million dollars, but to the average Nigerian, that's a gargantuan amount, in fact, it's beyond the scope of imagination for many of us.

Later that very month, bombs and rocket launchers were intercepted by security agencies at Apapa Wharf in Lagos. The papers would later report that the rocket launchers and bombs were allegedly misdirected to our country.

I am delighted that the security agencies managed to intercept the misdirected rockets before they would have "leaked" into the country. However, it's a shame that the general security situation in the country is not encouraging.

Effective but not efficient
I am very reluctant to join the bandwagon of those who blame the government for not doing enough to improve the security situation in the country. I am cautious because both the legislative and executive arm of the government did what was in their power by providing sufficient funds to support the security agencies in performing their roles. I am even more cautious because the presidents from time to time, especially since 1999, review the performances of security chiefs – across the army, navy, air force, the state security services and

the police – and make changes that they feel could improve the performances of the forces. I do not think that a president, or the legislature, would ordinarily think there was more they could do than these.

Imagine if you were the president, and the country was planning a less-than-2-days celebration of the 50th anniversary of independence. You invite the service chiefs and ask them what they would need to provide security for the events. They submit to you a bill of 500 million Naira – equivalent to 2 million pounds sterling. You send the bill to the National Assembly and it is approved. You get the accountant general to release the funds. You have provided what the service chiefs informed you that they would need to meet the security requirements – 2 million pounds sterling for a less-than-2-days event. Wouldn't you feel you have done enough to ensure security? Of course, you probably would. Moreover, you might well realise that some of the service chiefs have been in their respective professions while you, the president, were still a university undergraduate, with more than 25 years of security wisdom under each of their caps. I took an in-depth look at this perspective after I encountered some people blaming the president for not doing enough to improve the security of the country.

Today, the electorate debate between ourselves the issue of internal security in the country as we face the choice of electing one amongst four major candidates for the office of the president. One of them is a retired soldier who had been a coup plotter and Head of State; one is a retired police officer and former head of an anti-financial crimes agency; one is a mathematician who has been a state governor for 8 years and was the son of a police officer; and the other one is a former university don, a zoologist who was born to canoe makers and had been at various times, deputy governor, acting governor, governor, vice president, acting president, and is of course the incumbent president. I would think that to choose one amongst these four as the man who would be ultimately responsible for security in the country for the next four years would be very tricky. Some would say a retired soldier would be most effective, others would say a retired police officer would be most appropriate, yet others would say a mathematician who was brought up by a police officer would be most calculating, and yet others would argue that an academic person is always more analytical than others. Because I have stated that I should be politically neutral in public, I shall refrain from disclosing my preference amongst them in this matter, although I do admire the discipline of soldiers, the courage of the police, the intelligence of mathematicians, and deeply respect the analytical nature of academic minds.

I mentioned earlier that I do not think there was more the incumbent president would think he could have done, at least for security, during the 50th anniversary celebrations than he did. He probably did his best. I remember though that it had been said to me before "your best is not enough", when I had done my best in a particular situation. I have learnt since then, to use the argument "I did the best" – implying the best anyone in my situation would have done – rather than, "I did my best".

I thought I won't have the guts to say this, but I dare – the basic truth is that the security services in Nigeria are effective but not efficient.

I thought I won't have the guts to say this, but I dare – the basic truth is that the security services in Nigeria are effective but not efficient. With what the whole world saw happening close to our Eagles Square last October, I would think that for less than half the amount spent on providing security for that brief period, the security services could have done a more efficient job.

The problem, however, is that the entire security services system in the country would need to be completely overhauled first before we would see such efficiency but such an overhaul would come at a huge cost the country may not be willing to spend upfront.

Overhauling our police and justice system

I had been visiting a friend at Ibadan recently and had taken a walk one evening. I passed by a T-junction and noticed a police van that had apparently developed a fault. Its bonnet was open and two of the policemen were trying to fix it. I engaged the video camera function of my mobile phone and casually held it such that I could record the scene without being noticed. I did that successfully. Minutes later the men had fixed the noisy, aging Toyota Hilux pick-up van and managed to catch up with a group of political agents walking ahead. It dawned on me they had been probably charged with providing security cover for those people. The people held brooms in their hands as they sang along the street and stopped here and there pasting A2 size paper posters on the walls of private homes and fences, without requesting the permission of the home owners. It's normal in Nigeria. I reflected on the fact that using a noisy, aging pick-up van that might need to be fixed at several stops on a brief journey, is probably not the best way to provide security cover during political campaigns in a volatile city.

My thoughts drifted 9 years backwards to December 2001. In this same city, Ibadan, our country had lost the then Minister of Justice and Attorney-General of the Federation. The papers reported back then that the security agents charged with protecting him had been excused from his residence just before the murder took place. As of today, nobody has been convicted for that murder.

That slain Minister of Justice, the Late Chief Ajibola Ige, wanted to overhaul the administration of justice in Nigeria. In a letter purportedly written by him to former president Obasanjo, he had mentioned this. However, we do not know the nature or extent of the reforms he had in mind.

. . . the highest priority for the country at this time is not potable water or good roads or electricity. The highest priority is an overhaul of the system of our administration of justice.

Take it or leave it, the highest priority for the country at this time is not potable water or good roads or electricity. The highest priority is an overhaul of the system of our administration of justice. I had stated this earlier, and will have to reiterate it here – the weakness of the law is our bane. If you will not call my ideas childish and puerile, I will make recommendations here that we should seriously canvass for, when the new government is formed in May, irrespective of whoever emerges as president.

One of the very first things the president that would be sworn in this year should do is to overhaul the entire structure and operations of the justice system in the country, which includes the police, the courts, and the correctional facilities. They all go together. If we reform the police and the prisons, but leave out the courts, the system will not work and nothing in the country would work. If we reform the courts and prisons but leave out the police, the system would still be a failure. All the three would need to be reformed. But then you will ask, what does reforming the police, the courts and the prisons have to do with golden bombs and misdirected rockets? Everything. Reforms will bring about a total change.

Equipping the Police

I always appreciate good gifts. It is typical in Nigeria for state governors to donate crime fighting equipment to the Nigeria police every now and then. In fact, it is becoming fashionable – in the sense, of "just fashion". I do not doubt the effectiveness of the crime-fighting equipments which are usually pick-up vans (often Toyota Hilux with not-so-comfortable-looking straight-back benches put at the back for policemen to sit under trampoline covers. Some governors would add bullet-proof vests and communication gadgets. Whenever I see these acts, I wonder if the Governors think they have thus done enough to fight armed robbery, kidnapping, bomb blasts, rape, fraud, arson, etc in their states. I wonder how pick-up vans deter fraud, or rape, for instance. With all due respect to their Excellencies, I would think the country needs to fast forward into the present century. It's a shame that the Nigeria Police is run as though we are in the year 1914. If we can't fast forward to 2011, we should at least fast forward to 2010.

Don't get me wrong, I like the Nigeria Police. They say they are our friends and indeed I have friends, and relatives, and former school mates, who are officers in the Police. I remember walking into a station and meeting an old friend who told me he was there as an ASP-in-training (ASP is Assistant Superintendent of Police). He had graduated from the University of Ibadan with a degree in Psychology. I envied him. That's a good job and a good position. When I am with such policemen, I am comfortable that I am with my friends; and I am comfortable simply because we have been friends before they joined the police. If they had already joined the police before I knew them, it's most likely we won't ever be friends; or if ever we become friends, I won't be comfortable with them. I know the police are our friends. No doubt. But do you have anyone you cannot but keep as a friend? Say, like Matthew who lives next door and has a bad temper and could lose it at any time but is always ready to give you a helping hand whenever you need it? You know those kinds of friends? The type you would have cut off every relationship with if not because you find them useful, helpful, and rather dependable when you call on them? That's the kind of friends the Nigeria Police are to the Nigerian public. You don't really like them, but you don't hate them either – like a woman's cheating lover who is always there for her and watching her back. She knows he cares for her, he brings her gifts and pays her bills, but she just wonders why there's always the scent of another woman on him every time he comes to her. Yet he would swear by the heavens and the earth that he is faithful to her. She knows that he cheats but she just can't prove it. And if she cares prove it? She'd be ready for good slaps.

Somehow, I think the Nigeria Police are trained to slap indiscriminately.

Hmmn. Slaps. I told you about the policeman who slapped a guy who was waiting for a bus at the junction in Ibadan. Somehow, I think the Nigeria Police are trained to slap indiscriminately. My friend "Jalingo" was telling me the other day how two young policemen had accosted him and demanded for the purchase receipt of the laptop computer he had in his bag. He didn't have the receipt and they wanted to take him to the police station. They were not wearing the police uniform and he had demanded they should identify themselves before he would ride with them on their motorbike – which had no police identification – to the station. Of course, they gave him their identity – a clean slap. Another day, I was at a police station and I witnessed a policeman slapping an accused thief. He told the accused, *"You should thank your stars that my colleague 'So-and-so' is not around. If he slapped you, your ear would bleed"*. I didn't show my surprise. How could a policeman boast that his colleague batters an accused? Are we supposed to be guilty until proven innocent, or rather, innocent until proven guilty? And even at that, would a judge order penalty by slapping?

It didn't seem bad to any of the other policemen – and women – that were there. They had to do everything that would make the accused confess his acts. They have seen it happen many times. Accused young men would keep denying their complicity in a crime but after several slaps, they would confess. This method hasn't often failed the police. So, what's wrong with it? Slaps are very effective equipment for making accused persons confess. *Haba*.

In my humble opinion, I think Nigerian policemen need to be better equipped "internally" as much as they are equipped externally. Sometimes, these noble men do things that reduce your admiration of the great work they normally do. For instance, I had travelled to London with my laptop – and didn't bother taking the purchase receipt for it with me all the way. I went through customs and in a foreign land without being questioned about the proof of ownership of the laptop. But here in Nigeria, in my own country, most times I have to go with the receipt wherever the laptop goes. I was travelling to Ikole Ekiti last September and was stopped by a policeman at a checkpoint in Ado Ekiti.

Policeman:	What's in that bag on your back seat?
Me:	My computer.
Policeman:	A laptop? Are you with the receipt?
Me:	Yes, a laptop but no, I am not with the receipt. (*I wondered what other type of computer would fit into a slim bag if not a laptop*).
Policeman:	I will have to retain the computer here until you bring the receipt.
Me:	God! I don't usually take the receipt to work because I work and live on a University campus. I don't go through checkpoints, so I don't carry the receipt when I go to work. Today, I closed from work and directly embarked on this journey, I didn't think about taking the receipt. (*I brought out the University Staff ID Card*).

Policeman:	You work with a University? Well, you are lucky. If it were a business man, you won't leave here without paying at least 5000 Naira.
Me:	Thank you, sir. (*I wondered how paying 5000 Naira would normally replace his intended use of the receipt*). But by the way, why do you people always ask for the receipt of laptops? There are mobile phones that are more expensive than laptops and I would think that phones are easier to steal than laptops. Why don't you guys demand for phone receipts too? (*I smiled – I have learnt to always smile and make it sound like a joke when I ask sensitive questions that I think may offend. And that's also why several parts of this book have been deliberately put into a childish and jocular form*).
Policeman:	Oh, there are instances we could demand for receipt of mobile phones.
Me:	In fact, mobile phones are not the only examples, some people wear imported high-priced shoes that are more expensive than some laptops. Why don't you guys always demand for shoes receipts too? (*I smiled still and remained deliberately jocular*).
Policeman:	*Oga*, You can go now. Safe journey.
Me:	Thank you, sir. I'm most grateful.

At other times, I have been asked funnier questions by the police, which leave me wondering whether they were being deliberately mischievous or just plainly "natural".

Once I was driving my sister's car and I was stopped at a police check point. The policeman demanded for the vehicle papers and my driver's licence and I gave them to him. He soon noticed that my licence reads "Mr. Oyetomi" but the car papers read "Miss Oyetomi". He asked if the car belongs to my wife. I answered *"no, it's my sister's"* but I thought to myself, *"if I am Mr. Oyetomi, how do you expect my wife to be a Miss. Oyetomi"*? I smiled. I would later reflect and conclude that the gentleman must have been trying to set an intelligent trap for me. That was a generous conclusion. At other times, I would rather believe that he was just being natural and should have been better equipped internally to know how not to ask such "natural" questions.

Honestly, the equipment the Nigeria Police needs now more than any others are intelligence facilities. I have listened to the campaigns of the presidential candidates and they do mostly promise to reform the police but they simply fail to highlight exactly how they would do that.

Most Nigerian police stations are archaic. New ones being built are still fashioned after those ancient patterns. A word flashed across my mind now – REBRANDING. Prof. Dora Akunyilli, our immediate past Minister of Information and now a Senatorial candidate made that word more popular in the country. We need to rebrand the police and the entire justice system.

Rebranding the Police
You see, a typical police station in Nigeria is usually a small bungalow. Possibly the only office in there with a semi-functional air-conditioner would be that of the DPO (Divisional Police Officer) who heads that station. It's likely there will be no computers at all. If you find any, it might be the personal laptops of the officers or just one desktop computer used by the secretary to the DPO for typing letters. It would most likely be an old Pentium III, 128 MB RAM machine. Records of complaints and cases would be kept in paper files, possibly inside some wooden wardrobes or rusty metal cabinets. If a particular Governor were accused of having been an ex-convict and you ask the police to verify the information, they would have to comb through pages of paper files in some old stores to try and trace the records.

We would thank God if and when they find such files. But then, you would be surprised. The police might be asked to confirm the identity of that Governor, say one Jimmy Onadele Iboju. The police would say they have the record of one Jimmy O. Iboju who was prosecuted 6 years back but they are unable to confirm if the Jimmy O. Iboju of their own records is the same as the Jimmy O. Iboju that is now a Governor (or, should I say ex-Governor). You would wonder what happens to mug shots, or fingerprints, or audio/video recording of the investigations. But just as you are wondering, the newspapers would say the following day that even the case file found the previous day is now "missing". The third day, the Police would say it isn't missing. (I hope I won't get seriously slapped or maimed for these stuff I'm saying – because I'm not making it up. It actually happens every now and then).

See, some years back, I usually passed in front of a police station close to where I lived then. I noticed the police station does not appear to have adequate office space. Apart from the bungalow that housed the DPO's office, and the counter, and possibly the detention cell, the station has two auxiliary "offices". One of these auxiliary offices is just a shed – concrete floor, no walls at all, a roof of aluminium sheets on top of metal poles at the four angles, no ceiling. The gentlemen would sit on wooden benches. Mostly discussing, or playing a draught game while waiting probably for their next assignment. One of them is called "station guard". He has a rifle. He is always alert even when he appears to be absorbed in the discourses or draught game around him. How do I know he is always alert? I know, because if you strayed into the premises of the police station and move towards the bungalow, he would accost you. *"Yes, you, what do you want?"*, he would challenge you, nearly ferocious, never smiling. *"Sir, I lost my wallet and I want to make a police report"*, you would answer. *"Okay. Enter that place"*. He would point you to a small office, where you would meet policewomen – possibly secretaries – working in a small office with 2 or 3 tables so closely packed together they would need to squeeze themselves in-between to pass. The secretary would take a copy of an affidavit you had gone to swear in court and prepare a police statement from it on a mechanical typewriter – the type that were most popular in the 1960s.

The other auxiliary office outside the bungalow is a small wooden structure built near the concrete fence of the private property next-door to the police station. The only concrete side of that office is the fence itself. The other three sides are made from timber planks with signs of extensive termite infestation. The floor is the reddish brown soil of the earth, no concrete, no cement. The roof also is simply sheets of aluminium. No ceiling. No fans. A policewoman of middle rank – actually an Inspector – seats on a plastic chair for official duties – the type Nigerians usually use at *Owambe* parties – and her desk, a small plastic table about 3 feet by 2 feet. She prepares her reports and case notes under these conditions. I did use the camera function of my phone to quietly record all these while I was with them. I thought to myself, no wonder the police are our "compulsory" friends. How could a woman who has served in the police for possibly 15 to 20 years be entitled to an office no better than this, working under the harsh heat that averages 32 degrees Celsius every day! Why won't policemen working under such stressful conditions transform the heat that beats upon their heads into slaps on the face of the accused persons? Just this past week, I deliberately drove past that particular station to be sure the scenario had not changed before I sent this to press. I can bet now, if you go there right now, it is still the same!

> No ceiling. No fans. A policewoman of middle rank – actually an Inspector – seats on a plastic chair for official duties
> . . .

I pitied the officers. I admired them at once. For them to keep working under these inhumane conditions, the Nigeria policemen should be praised daily. In computer science, we call something "garbage in, garbage out". As I moved away from that station, I noticed there's a large private building opposite the station. That building, a duplex, has security cameras on the outside. The police station directly opposite it does not have any. I thought to myself, what a parody!

And yet we do not expect bombs to blast off near Eagles' Square. What's the Police Service Commission doing about all this? What's the Ministry of Police Affairs doing? What are the Committees on Police Affairs in both the Senate and House of Representatives doing? Do they ever take a tour of police stations across the country to see the working conditions here and there and look for ways to improve them?

The Police Equipment Fund

Just now, I remembered there were in the not-too-distant past some newspaper coverage of contentions about how 50 Billion Naira (that's 200 million pounds) Police Equipment Fund was spent. I have checked the website of the Nigeria Police Force, trying to find information about how many police stations there are in the country, but I couldn't get that information. I know the country has less than 800 local government areas. And I know I live in a large local government area. I do not think we have up to 60 police stations in this local government. If there are 60 police stations in 800 local governments, we would still have less than 50,000 police stations across the country.

So, what would I do if I were Kenny Martins, former chairman of the Police Equipment Fund? Would I have bought and distributed vehicles like he did? Certainly not. Divide 50 billion Naira into 50,000 places and you will get at least 1 million per police station. What would 1 million Naira do in each police station? Plenty. Actually, I won't equip the police stations on an individual basis. Rather, I would build a large electronic network and link every police station in Nigeria to a secure electronic network. I know there's electricity problem in Nigeria and would put a generator in every police station. I would put a VSAT equipment to link each station to the internet. I would put computers in each police station with finger print reading equipment. Then I would ensure there's a large and robust Police Headquarters in Abuja which would function like the headquarters of banks in Nigeria. Banks, like First Bank Nigeria Plc and UBA successfully link their branches nationwide electronically, and process millions of transactions

I pitied the officers. I admired them at once. For them to keep working under these inhumane conditions, the Nigeria policemen should be praised daily.

91

electronically every day, while transferring the cost of keeping their networks running in the face of chronic erratic electric power supply to their customers. Can't our country do the same with the Police force and transfer the cost to us, taxpayers. And for that matter, I won't limit myself to 50 Billion Naira.

You know it is a tall talk, if I should say such things like "if I were the president". I know I can't be and I do not intend to be. But just if I were the president that Nigerians would vote in April and swear in on May 29, 2011, one of the very first things I would do is send a bill proposing reforms of the Police formation across the country. I would actually send a request to the National Assembly to approve the spending of N1.5 trillion (10 billion US dollars) on reforming the Nigerian police over a 3 year period. It would be N500 billion per year. You say Nigeria cannot afford that? Of course, what we pay in terms of losses of human life and property, and looting of the "national cake", is more than this.

How could a woman who has served in the police for possibly 15 to 20 years be entitled to an office no better than this, working under the harsh heat that averages 32 degrees Celsius every day!

The first year, I would propose a 100 billion National Police Academy. I would ensure it is completed within 2 years and would fund it at 50 billion for each of the first 2 years. The Police Academy would serve as a ground for continuous in-service training of police officers. I would procure about 100 helicopters at about 50 Billion, or less, and spread them across the most crime ridden arrears of the country.

If there is sufficient police helicopter coverage for the country, we would have less kidnapping and bombings. I doubt if the entire Nigeria Police Force has up to 10 helicopters at present. Actually, I have never seen a police helicopter in this country. Have you ever seen one?

Last July, when armed robbers invaded

Akure and operated in 2 banks right at the core of the city for more than 30 minutes, if there were police helicopters, say at least one permanently stationed in each senatorial district, the police could have pursued the armed robbers and monitored them from the air. The air unit would stay above, and give feeds on the ground movement of the fleeing robbers to police vehicles on the ground.

From the 400 billion Naira left for the first year (which would be averagely 8 million Naira per police station – on the assumption of 50,000 police stations), I would first provide a "Police Link Unit" in police station across the country. The Police Link Unit would be an office equipped within each station to link to a central police office electronically. I'd put a VSAT internet link, with a 100 KVA power generator, at least 10 computers, finger printing equipment, and cameras. I would add a 10 KVA power inverter to power the "Police Link Unit" such that they won't need to run the generator round the clock. Mostly, the generator would run at night, providing lighting for the station and power to charge the inverters. During the day, the generators would not be in use. Power stored in the inverters would power the police link.

Then I would take care of only the highest priority renovations in each police station across the country. For instance, do the concrete flooring of the bare-earth auxiliary offices and replace termite-infested wooden office walls with decent brick walls. Improve ventilations with fans and reduce the heat of the roofs with ceilings. There would be room to improve the conduciveness of the stations over the next 2 years. But my priority in the first year would be the police link.

What's the use of the police link? Good question. It would serve for information and intelligence sharing across the entire police formation in the country. If a car is reported stolen at Ijapo police station, the report would be immediately logged into the police link. Every police station across the country would immediately have that information. If a bank robbery takes place at Oshodi, immediately it's reported, it will be logged and every police station across the country would have that information.

However, the greatest use of the police link would be "case history management". If a case of rape is reported at Lafenwa police station in

Abeokuta, the desk officer would input the name of the accused into the police link network and see if he has had any history with the police. The Lafenwa station would be able to know within minutes that the young man had been previously reported at Eleweran police station over similar charges in the past.

With the police link, the Inspector General of the Police can have a firsthand review of any case anywhere in the country from his office. When a newspaper reporter calls the Force PRO about a kidnapping case in Anamabra, the Force PRO would not have to give the excuse that he has not been briefed by the Commissioner of Police in Anambra, who would in turn say he has not been briefed by a DPO. Once any case is reported at any police station, the information becomes accessible through a secure network at all police stations across the country. There would be levels of access to view the information. The police as a formation could easily analyse crime data and patterns in real time. The IG in his office could say, a total of 10 arsons have been reported across the country between 8 am and 9 am this morning. The force PRO could say most rape cases occur at Ajegunle and between 6 pm and 9 pm on weekends. The police academy could regularly brainstorm and analyse how to solve these problems using reliable and up-to-the-minute data.

As president, I would ask the Police to get a national emergency number, say 419 like the Americans use 911. It won't be various numbers for various police stations. I saw some very long un-memorisable numbers on the website of the Nigerian police. How on earth do they expect anyone to know such numbers? The first thing most robbers do now is to take your phone from you so you won't be able to call. How does the Nigerian police expect a traumatised robbery victim, whose phone has been taken from him, to remember a 10-digit emergency number? It's rather ridiculous. I mean, we could instead have 419 – which is the most popular police code in Nigeria. If you are robbed, and your phone is taken, you can get to a call centre and just dial 419.

As part of the police link, I would ask Glo telecoms, being the Second National Carrier licensed, to provide a switchboard line 419 to the Nigerian police headquarters (NITEL the first National Carrier licensee is hibernating presently). Or, I could ask the various telecoms operators in the country to bid for it. The 419 line will be toll-free irrespective of phone network from which the call originates. There will be mandatory recording of all calls to the switchboard. When a call comes in to the switchboard, a police operator will take the complaints, or report, and immediately forward directions to the nearest police station for action. There will automatically be a record of the exact moment a victim made a call to the 419 line to report a crime. There will be record of the exact moment the police operator made contact with the nearest police station. It will be possible to investigate any negligence or undue delay. These are not tall dreams, these are what are taken for granted in the democracy we copied, and we can afford it!

I mean our government can give 500 billion Naira bailout fund to banks, 200 billion bailout fund to the textile industry, 200 billion Naira agric loan guarantee to farmers, but have not thought about a N200 billion Naira police link to connect all police stations in the country into one single intelligence gathering force. Does it mean we cannot afford it?

If I were the president, the second year, I would complete the Police Academy with 100 Billion Naira. I would upgrade half of the 50,000 police stations in the country structurally. Instead of "counters" where belligerent looking and harsh speaking policemen sit, I would actually make the front desk of every police station look like the customer service centre desk of banks and telecoms centres. Have you been to the MTN service centre at the Mobil bus-stop Ibadan? Actually, that's how a police station should look like. There should be friendly-faced police officers sitting behind computers in an air-conditioned customers' service unit. When you go in there to make enquiries or complaints, the police should attend to you courteously and welcome you with a smile – as though you are an old friend they have missed. There should be a public water dispenser where you can take a cup of cold water or warm if you prefer. There should be functional conveniences where you can ease yourself while you wait with them.

And that reminds me, I had needed to urinate once while waiting at a police station. The officer simply asked me to walk towards the back of the station building, and "urinate where you see those rubbish". It was a smelly place: paper refuse, empty plastic bottles, spent cans of soft drinks, evidence of continuous urination. It's a shame. See, if you win this next presidential election, whoever you are, I would not like to see such nauseating police stations when you are leaving office. I would want working environments where the police officers could proudly say, *"this is my office, this is where I work, would you like to come in and have a drink?"*

Have you noticed that kids growing up in Nigeria always want to be doctors, engineers, lawyers, nurses, ... soldiers possibly, but never policemen? Ooops. I have talked too much now. I don't want to say more lest I should imply that it's only those who have no other options that join the police in Nigeria. Actually, if you would recruit me, I might like to join – but I won't like a bare-earth office floor, or a van I would need to wait and check the bonnet of, while escorting political campaigners in a volatile neighbourhood. Much more, I won't like to sit face to face with a person who has extensive criminal records in other police stations in the country while I as an investigating police officer remain unaware of such records.

What's the highest priority?

When we were kids, we read books by the Late J. F. Odunjo. A genius writer and poet of Yoruba extracts, whose *Alawiye* books gave us insights into the wisdom of the ancients. In one of his stories, captioned *Ogbon Ologbon Ni Ko Je Ka Pe Agbalaba Ni Were* – (which might roughly translate as "borrowed wisdom reveals that the ancients are not fools") – Chief Odunjo told us of a wealthy man whose will mandated his only child to choose just one of his entire property, while the rest should be handed over to his principal slave.

That only child became saddened. He wondered why his father did him so much cruelty, allowing him to choose just one of his possessions, while the rest would be given to his slave. He hated his father's action so much. But one day luck smiled on him. An old wise man in the neighbourhood invited him for a talk and whispered something in his ears. Meanwhile, the slave went about rejoicing that he would inherit everything and become rich while his master's son would be poor. Alas, when the day came for the son to declare his choice, he chose just one of his father's possessions according to the will of his late father. His choice? He chose for a possession the very principal slave to whom every other possession was willed. The slave was devastated. He knew that whoever owns him owns all his belongings. The young man had used the borrowed wisdom of the sage to choose right.

So, when our president is sworn in on May 29, 2011, what should be the primal request we should make to him? Some folks say electricity. Some say potable water. Some say good roads. The list is endless. I still *dey* laugh at the way we prioritise these stuff. You may not like it, but this is what the "*Eternal Sage*" whispered in my ears – "*tell your country to fix the justice system and every other thing would be bonus to your land*".

Righteousness Exalts a Nation

I read the Bible not just for religious reasons. There is administrative guidance in the Bible too. When in Proverbs 14: 34, the Bible says, "*righteousness exalts a nation, but sin is a reproach to any people*", it wasn't only about religious righteousness. There's a "legal righteousness", which our nation has consistently ignored.

Every now and then, people complain about corruption. They would talk about the party that has ruled the country since 1999 and say it is a corrupt party. I would laugh. I bet you don't know what corruption is.

Corruption goes beyond diverting public funds into personal use. Have you ever had cause to seek assistance from an acquaintance who works in a firm and asked him or her to "use connections" to help you get a job with the firm? That's corruption. Have you ever given photocopies of your child's school results to a professor friend who works at a particular university to help your child secure admission into that university, while there are well-laid out examination-regulated entry modes? That's corruption. Have you ever had to buy a car "imported" (actually, smuggled), from Cotonou through the land border? That's corruption.

> Corruption goes beyond diverting public funds into personal use.

I don't want to give you an exhaustive list because I don't want you to see yourself as an abject sinner. But you see, I know many churches where even the Bible Study

97

outlines are prepared with pirated versions of Microsoft Office software, yet the pastors of these churches will tongue lash politicians for "corruption". Posters for religious programmes are designed with pirated versions of Corel Draw software, yet the religious leaders would talk about corruption.

See, a pastor friend suggested to me to "stop wasting money" paying internet subscription. He referred me to one of his friends who could get me MTN cheat codes, hack the MTN modem, so I could use the internet through the MTN network without paying subscriptions to the company. I told him, *"that's wrong"*. He didn't understand why or how it is wrong. I gave him the analogy that it is like going through a hole in the fence into a farm and stealing corn, then coming out to say *"why do you spend money buying corn, people go through a God-provided route at the back of the farm to get corn"*. He saw the point but I doubt if he was convinced. To many Nigerians, that's smartness not corruption. *"It's only the leaders that are corrupt. We should vote in the retired soldier because of his anti-corruption reputation. We should vote in the former head of the EFCC because of his anti-corruption reputation. Those who are eating money in Abuja are the corrupt ones. We are the saints."* It's a shame that kettles call pots black. Anyway, I agree with you that Nigeria's wealth should be better managed than it has been since 1960, and I will discuss that in details in the next chapter.

Chapter 7

Too Much Money, Problem is How To Spend It

Nigerian leaders stole $400bn between 1960 and 1999 - Prof. Akinyemi
The Nigerian Tribune, 30 April 2010.

Even the dogs

I was not yet born when General Yakubu Gowon was president. I have heard it many times that he once said that "*the problem with Nigeria is not money, but how to spend it*". Actually, I have seen Gowon in person only once. And that was this year at the 2nd Foundation Day Ceremony of the Afe Babalola University in Ado Ekiti. Gowon had been invited to deliver a lecture titled "*Alarming Decline in Education Standard in Nigeria: Reversing it and Moving Forward*". The Governor of Ekiti State Dr. Kayode Fayemi, in his brief comments, did mention this long-told story about Gowon saying Nigeria having much money with the problem of how to spend it. I cannot recollect any rebuttal of that fact by Gowon at that event, and for this, I would believe he may indeed have said so.

Actually, if you witness the way some Nigerians spend money – as though money is never earned, but just fetched from some streams flowing through their backyard gardens, you would not contend. I dedicate this book to both the incumbent head of state as well as "the many Nigerians who have less to eat than even the dogs of their rich neighbours" but I fear someone might think it's figurative. Actually, it's literal.

I was visiting a family in Ibadan some years back, and noticed they had a large store where cartons of tinned food were stored. I noticed in one partly-opened carton a can that I assumed was corned beef. I was delighted that I would return to school with some corned beef if my host would be generous enough to spare some cans. After all, he had a whole room packed full of it. However, I was soon corrected – "it's not corned beef, it's dog meal. We import and sell dogs, and the

99

canned meat meals are for the dogs". I think he said it was 380 Naira per can and a dog would take about 2 of it a day. If men lived for food only, I would have envied those dogs! Back then a University student could survive on 380 Naira for a whole week, and here were puppies living on twice as much as that daily!

See, whenever I say "corned beef", there are many Nigerians that look at my mouth wondering what "corned beef" means. It's true! They have no idea what it means. They've never seen it nor tasted it. Their family – father, mother, children and visiting cousins – would not spend as much as 760 on food in a day. Yet, *Lucky* the Alsatian dog, or *Bobby* the pit-bull terrier, have the luxury of eating imported canned meat worth that much daily. That was even 12 years ago, when the take home salaries of Professors – highest paid University workers – had just been reviewed upwards from 9000 Naira per month. Who knows whether those canned meat meals would be about 1000 Naira per can now.

Too Much Money, Problem is How to spend it.

I used to have a neighbour. All his children had grown up and left home. He and his wife were left to manage their 7 cars, which included 2 SUVs, and yet they still had official chauffeur-driven cars assigned to them from their respective offices. I wondered what was the use of having 9 cars at your disposal when you could, in fact, live conveniently with just 2. That family is not "wealthy", they are middle class Nigerians. As for the wealthy ones? The competition has shifted from how many cars are usually packed in their yards, or how many houses they have in the country, it has moved on to what position they occupy on the Forbes magazine list of billionaires in the world. It's not a bad idea, at least it gives us some good stock to brag about – Nigeria too is now represented on Forbes list. Hurray! *No be so?* Really, though, I would be more comfortable if the competition were for positions on the list of highest-tax-paying Nigerians.

Come, you won't like me for this – but I will tell you all the same – the problem with the Nigerian economy, and all the problems with the Nigerian society which most of us have been complaining about lies in just one fact– we are not a taxpaying economy. Unless and until Nigeria copies the taxpaying ideology and structure of the country whose form of government we copied, we shall remain with our problems.

Sometimes, I read in Nigerian newspapers and see some journalists mentioning "taxpayer money", in imitation of the Americans, and I wonder if they understand what "taxpayer" means. What percentage of the national budget is actually based on tax estimates? What percentage of the population pays taxes?

Nigeria indeed has too much money – in a manner of speaking. But if, indeed, the money is too much, why then do we not have everything we need? Why do we not have enough power supply, or potable water, or good roads, or excellent health facilities? If indeed we have too much money, why is our Federal Government budget just about $35 billion dollars a year – which is much less than a third of the $132 billion budget of New York State? Indeed, poor people have poor perspectives of life. When you give a poor man $100, he feels like a Governor. He would start singing *Yahooze* - "*too much money, problem is how to spend! Yahoo, oh oh, yahooze.*" It's actually a matter of poverty of ideas.

. . . the problem with the Nigerian economy, and all the problems with the Nigerian society which most of us have been complaining about lies in just one fact– we are not a taxpaying economy.

Why you dey vex? Is it your money?

I have seen it too many times. You find people mismanaging "Government money" and you try to protest but their bouncers and escorts will deal roughly with you. You can't just protest the fact that someone is diverting public funds and resources into his private use. It appears that the only times that such people get really dealt with is when they offend people who are higher than them in government, or when their superiors in government wish to use them as cheap point-scoring objects.

It's a shame that the same people amongst the masses who keep grumbling about corruption, in fact, expect political office holders and public servants to be corrupt. If you are a public servant or political office holder, and you keep living a low profile life, no big cars, no big houses, no extravagant parties – especially if while you are in office your child is marrying or you lose a parent – people would *yab* you and call you "stupid". Many Nigerians see it as smartness when you divert public funds successfully without being caught. They see it as stupidity when you have an opportunity to do it but refrain. Yet we want electricity and potable water and good roads.

See, *I suppose dey vex.* I should be very angry at the nation. No, not just at the leaders. I ought to be angry at the system. We have everything and live as though there's nothing. And if you will have it, I have every right to be angry. I don't like the "State and Local Government of Origin" methodology used in the country, it only serves to breed apathy. But if you would allow me to pursue that as most of us do, I will let you know that I am also from the Niger Delta. There are oil wells in my father's village. I doubt if most of you can say the same. And if you must know why I ought to be angry at the nation, you should see it from that fact.

If you wish to take a trip to my father's village, I will take you there. Most of the houses there are built from bamboo and roofed with raffia. Most of my folks don't have access to the "enjoyment" you have in the cities. I remember that some years back when a certain Group Managing Director of the Nigerian National Petroleum Corporation was removed from office, it was revealed he had spent four years at premium suites at a Hilton hotel, spending about 300,000 Naira per night. Most of you were shocked and angry that a single man had spent more than 240 million Naira on hotel bills. I would rudely put it to you that you were only angry, possibly, because in your own offices you didn't have such opportunities. I could bet that if you too had the same opportunities as that GMD had, you would have done the same.

Really, I must wonder why you *dey vex. We sef wey dem dey carry the oil kommot from our village no vex reach una.* You live in air conditioned, soft-carpet, marble-paved houses. Our fathers and cousins live inside bamboo huts and yet it is from our backyards and beneath the rivers that we drink that you get the funds to live large. Then when our boys get really angry at the imbalance in the society – and do what they shouldn't do – you call them militants.

Now, be careful. Do I support militancy? No, not at all. Do I support kidnapping of foreign oil workers in demand for ransom? No, not at all. Do, I support those who blow up oil pipelines? No, not at all. However, I would say that these same gentlemen you call "militants" were failed by the society. I grew up away from the village and had relatively better education than those my distant "cousins" in the creeks. Possibly, if they had the opportunity for better education as I did, they won't be "militants" today. However, if they are not "militants", what better options would they have?

See, many of those "militants" may have preferred to follow the non-violent activism of the late Ken Saro Wiwa of the Movement for the Survival of the Ogoni People. However, he was tried and killed under the administration of Sani Abacha – a killing that was seriously condemned by international communities and earned Nigeria a suspension from the Commonwealth.

I have been privileged to study the attitudes and behaviours of youths. Often times, the easiest way to entrench moral values in growing minds is to pass them through a system of rewards and punishment. They have to see evil being punished and good being rewarded. Unfortunately, our country has lapsed into a situation whereby good is punished and evil is rewarded. Non-violent activism earns state execution; violent activism earns state pardon and stipends. It's confounding.

The cake is not national enough.

I can't but keep referring to the National Geographic Wild channel. I find it interesting to watch animal behaviour and compare with how humans also behave. I had always heard of the proverbial lion share but didn't fully comprehend its true meaning until I saw it on the National Geographic channel.

You see, in the wild, the lionesses do most of the hunting. But when a kill is made, the dominant male in the pride feeds first. It consumes the largest and choicest portion of a kill it did not make. When I look at this country and see the approach of many people, especially public office holders, to the wealth of the nation, I am reminded of the behaviours of such wild animals. Sometimes I get tempted to say "*anü öhia*" – as my Igbo friends would say.

Here in Nigeria, our people – *my* people (to be more exact) – in the oil producing communities live in "houses" (actually bamboo huts) that don't cost more than 30,000 Naira to build – if you want a really large house, whereas people who have never seen an oil well since they were born earn allowances and salaries upwards of 15 000 000 Naira per month.

> *The real militants are those who are blowing up the minds of the youths in the creeks and kidnapping their dreams and visions.*

I bet the reason some people vote the lion share of the national cake to themselves is just because they don't take part in the kill. The baking of the national cake is not national enough. The South-South produces the most of the country's wealth, yet it is arguably the least developed region of the country. I would rather think that the real militants are not those who are blowing up pipelines and kidnapping oil workers. The real militants are those who are blowing up the minds of the youths in the creeks and kidnapping their dreams and visions. This is not a justification for violence, though. It is only a pointer to where the real problem lies.

Of course, I must add that, although the incumbent president is also from the South-South and he is running now to be elected as president this year, I am not bringing these issues up as a justification for him to be voted in as president. I have said it before and I will repeat here, when it comes to elections, I cannot tell you who to vote for or not. Besides, I no longer see the president as belonging to the South-South. He is now a Federal citizen. Once a man becomes the president of a country, ideally, he should lose his local identity and assume a national one. In reality, this may not always be the case, but I will stick with my ideals.

Now back to what I was saying: people in government spend money too recklessly in this country and sometimes lay an "official claim" to doing so. If you don't mind, I would like to suggest that before the members of the Senate and House of Representatives are sworn in into office, they should be allowed to take a retreat to the oil producing villages of Nigeria and live with our people for just a weekend. Let them drink the waters from the streams that we drink – not the carefully bottled water they drink in Abuja. Let them sleep in our bamboo and raffia huts and be bitten by *otongbolo* (aggressive mosquitoes). Let them feel the standard and quality of life of the oil producing communities for just a weekend. Before going to Abuja to assume the role of sharing the national cake, they should first come to the "kitchen" and feel the heat of "the oven".

> *Unfortunately, people in leadership positions are so focused on the oil earnings of the country that they have little or no time to think about taxes.*

I have often heard from many people that *"there is just too much money in this country. The money dey there, dem just dey chop am!"* Actually, it makes me wonder whose money they are talking about. The country's money? No, more exactly the money from our villages and creeks.

The proper way to turn this country around is to make a shift from the oil economy to a taxpayer economy. That's the only thing that can stop corruption and bring peace into the country. Everybody should contribute via taxes. If there is an effective tax administration in the country, the present oil earnings of the country would only account for less than 20 percent of the country's earnings. Unfortunately, people in leadership positions are so focused on the oil earnings of the country that they have little or no time to think about taxes.

Democracies are financed by taxes, not oil.
Look around the world, you will see that most of the successful democracies in the world are financed by taxes and not oil.

Let's do some scenario planning management. There is a question I would really like to put to the present presidential candidates:

> *Suppose something terrible happens in May 2011, and the international community puts sanctions on Nigerian oil for the next four years, no single barrel of oil is to be lifted or sold, throughout the four years, how would you run this country?*

Most likely, the answer I would get would be *"God forbid. That cannot happen. It won't happen by God's grace".* So, where is creative thinking?

> *. . . any person who cannot come up with a logical answer on how to finance and govern this country effectively for the next four years without a single kobo coming from oil is not competent to govern this country.*

See, any person who cannot come up with a logical answer on how to finance and govern this country effectively for the next four years without a single kobo coming from oil is not competent to govern this country. Take it or leave it.

There are some facts I need to draw to your attention. Are you aware that Canada is also an oil producing country? Do you know that Canadian oil reserves are about 5 times that of Nigeria? Nigeria has an estimated 360 billion barrel reserve whereas Canada has nearly 1800 billion barrels. Do you know that the daily oil production of Canada and Nigeria are about the same? Yet at that rate Nigeria's oil has a reserve life of 40 years, while Canada's is about 180 years. Yet less than 20% of the Canadian federal budget comes from oil.

Just now I recollect how I mentioned to some folks that the oil reserves of Nigeria has a life span estimated at 40 years and they laughed at me. I was telling them that in 40 years time, Nigeria's oil well would be dry. No more oil money to share as national cake. But they derided me – *"Temitope has come again with his fake ideas. Oil dry up ke? Oil can never dry up. It is God that has put it there. It can never finish."* Poor folks.

You don't understand. We have already eaten the larger part of the cake! Our country started producing oil in commercial quantities in 1956 – that is some 54 years ago, our reserves are now estimated at 40 years. It means on a scale of 94 years, we have already taken out 54. We have eaten (or wasted) the greater part of the cake! You better start thinking of tomorrow. And tomorrow starts today. It starts now.

The time for the country to close her eyes to the oil, and ignore it, and present a budget totally financed without oil earnings is now. That's what I am waiting to see.

See, the United States of America whose form of democracy we copied is a tax-driven economy. Most people in America don't dread the police, but they dread the IRS – Internal Revenue Service. One of the easiest ways to go to jail in America is to evade tax or not pay it correctly.

Nigerians are not tax payers[11]. The few people who pay income taxes in Nigeria are people employed by the government, or banks, and well-organised private corporations. It's a farce. If the government pays you 100,000 per month and then turns around to tax you 2000 Naira, that's not taxpaying. The government may as well have paid you 98,000 Naira tax-free in the first place.

I sat in a barber's shop one evening. Guys were coming in to get barbed and were paying 200 Naira per cut. Right there, in my presence, at least 7 guys were attended to before it was my turn. I estimated that this gentleman would barb for 30 to 50 people per day and earn about 6000 to 10 000 Naira gross. Does he pay income taxes? I don't think so. Do you know that some directors in State Government services actually earn less than barbers and *okada* riders? (An *okada* is a motorcycle used as taxi).

---

[11] http://en.wikipedia.org/wiki/Economy_of_Nigeria

An *okada* rider told me he got a bike on hire purchase and was to pay 100,000 in 10 instalments over a 10 week period. He told me he was putting aside 1500 Naira every evening from Mondays to Saturdays and 1000 Naira on Sundays. That's after he would have deducted his running costs for the day and would have had a "take-home" allowance to live on. It was a casual talk. He was sharing with me about his disappointment with another friend of his that he had similarly helped to acquire an *okada*. But he didn't know he was opening my eyes to an interesting fact – I was saying in me "So, you guys make so much money from *okada*! How much tax do you pay?"

Every time I bring this up, I get shouted down. People would tell me, "*You want to compound the suffering of the masses. The people you are suggesting that government should tax are suffering and sweating*". But the truth is that people who do similar jobs elsewhere also pay taxes. The Nigerian tax administration should be completely overhauled.

Social Security and Tax Identification
In the United States they have what is called the Social Security Number (SSN). That number doubles as a taxpayer identification number. There is the equivalent of it for corporations. It's called Employer Identification Number (EIN). You cannot open a bank account in the US without a taxpayer identification number be it as an individual or as a corporation. You cannot have your vehicle licensed without it. That is the democracy whose form of government we copied.

If the Nigerian government is bold enough to copy that form of tax administration, it will solve many problems in the country. It will curb corruption and armed robbery and violence. For example, at present, you would normally see some civil servants who earn 100 000 Naira per month buying cars worth 3 000 000 Naira in cash, and owning houses worth 6 000 000 Naira!

It has even been alleged that some civil servants have up to 12 billion Naira in their accounts and own scores of petrol stations. An effective taxpayer identification number system would make it easy to detect all that stuff. If people can't get a licence for their petrol station without a taxpayer identification number, if they can't buy a car or build a house without one, if they can't transfer funds abroad without it, there would be considerable reduction in corruption.

Talk about *Yahoo-Yahoo* too; if people can't collect Western Union Money Transfer without their taxpayer identification number, it will make a big difference.

Smuggling and kidnapping? An effective taxpayer identification system would fix that. See, if someone kidnaps, say a commissioner's mother, and collects a 5 million Naira ransom, if he cannot buy a car with it, or build a house, or set up a business, or lodge it into a bank account, or transfer it abroad, you would have rendered his 5 million Naira mostly useless. So, the most effective way to control kidnapping is not by deploying soldiers to the streets of the south-east and south-south, when you tighten financial loopholes, and there is little people can do with money unless through the eyes of the police and tax administrations, kidnapping will be drastically cut down.

And with taxes, you can even correct the anomalies of the past. There are the leaders of yesterday and their collaborators who are alleged to have stolen more than 400 billion dollars between 1960 and 1999 and mismanaged another 400 billion dollars thereafter. Big money, but not a big deal. A simple progressive tax can correct that. Progressive tax means we won't all pay the same rates of tax. Our Nigerian billionaires on the Forbes list should pay taxes at higher rate than others.

I once met a woman who claims to own 76 petrol stations. I guess she doesn't pay as much tax as a University professor and yet she is rich enough to employ the professor if she so wishes.

Do any of the present presidential candidates have a vision to overhaul the tax administration of the country? Have they mentioned this in their campaigns? I'm waiting to hear that.

This is one reason I have not been voting. I have not found the level of creativity demonstrated by the erstwhile candidates stimulating enough to attract my vote. However, I shall vote this year, not because the present gentlemen who are desiring to become president have learnt to talk about tax reforms but just because after voting I would have the guts to talk directly to anyone who emerges as president about tax reforms and what I think the man should do to urgently move the country forward. Trust me, I won't be doing the back-of-the-classroom grumbling that most of us do. I would directly write to the president and tell him what I need him to do for the country. It will cost me only a few sheets of paper and the equivalent of less than 5 pounds postage. Do you know what back-of-the-classroom grumbling means? It's a way of *yabbing* the teacher when you are among your friends at the back of the class. You say terrible things about the teacher and mock her. She doesn't hear what you are saying. Your friends hear you, and giggle; the teacher wonders what's funny and is frustrated that you are distracting her class. But you are too chicken to say out loud and clear to her hearing what you say at the back of the class. Many of us in Nigeria do the same with the government. We stand back and say all sorts of things about governors and presidents, some of us are bold enough to put some nasty ones in newspapers but if it comes to looking eye to eye with the president or governors and senators, we chicken out. I think I have found only one man in Nigeria, that's Sanusi Lamido Sanusi, who has guts and demonstrated it. Why is he not a Senator or Rep.? That's the kind of guy I'd like to vote for, if he has a listening ear in additional to being bold and sincere.

Electricity, Good Roads, Water Supply and Health.

Our immediate past president, the late Umaru Y'aradua, is possibly one of the best among the men that have governed this country. He had a vision. He had a good heart. But he didn't have a good health. He came on board and declared a seven point agenda. People say that was audacious. Even Sanusi Lamido Sanusi, whose frankness I admire, spoke against the impracticability of Y'aradua's 7-point agenda. On that one note, I would disagree with Sanusi.

You see, a 7-point agenda is not over-ambitious. It's realistic and achievable. The problem was that it was not properly highlighted and planned and worked out.

For all I know, the way to get things done is not by just listing what you desire to do. Your agenda is only proper when it highlights costs and time-frames for each piece of work to be done and pin-points who would be responsible and accountable for each assignment and details the penalty for the failure to carry out the assignment.

I watched some of our presidential candidates campaigning before the primaries and couldn't help but laugh. They were talking about electricity, good roads, water supply and health. Yeah, all these stuff matter very seriously.

If you must know, no one feels the brunt of lack of these things more than I do. Talk about good roads, I have had road accidents many times, including twice in which I had serious fractures. Talk about electricity, my businesses have been negatively affected and nearly brought to complete halt for lack of adequate electricity. There was a particular day I had borrowed 10,000 Naira from a friend and used everything to buy petrol for the generator, just so I could have power supply to work with. Talk about water supply, I know what that means. In my father's village, you don't have to shower; you go to the river to bath. You bath downstream and go upstream to fetch the water you drink. But then, what's "upstream" to you is also "downstream" to some other people, and in reality, you are drinking what other people have washed their bodies and dirty clothes into and defecated into, and this is untreated. Yet that's where the oil is extracted for some people, who have never suffered in life; they drink water only if it is bottled water, amongst other luxuries.

. . . the way to get things done is not by just listing what you desire to do. Your agenda is only proper when it highlights costs and time-frames for each piece of work to be done and pin-points who would be responsible and accountable . . .

Talking about health, I have witnessed firsthand the ugly side of the health sector in Nigeria. When I had that accident in 2008, and was hospitalised at a Federal Medical Centre, I witnessed how lack of adequate

111

facilities hinder the hospitals from doing the best they can do. I already mentioned how in the 2001 accident, no x-rays were taken for 2 full days after I was rescued from the accident scene, and how it was I that informed the hospital that I had a hidden fracture rather than the other way around. At FMC in 2008, I saw guys who were amputated on credit. They couldn't afford to pay for the procedure. They already owed the hospital but then their cases were urgent and the hospital had to do something immediately. I remember meeting a guy who worked as a commercial bus driver. He had an accident. His right arm had been amputated following the accidents. Weeks later, the hospital decided to amputate the right leg. He couldn't afford to pay for the second operation. I overheard the doctors telling him they would do it for him and he could come back to pay the bills afterwards.

There was a guy whose bed was directly opposite mine. He was a victim of electrocution. He had no feeling in his legs any more. He looked so pale. The doctors wanted to do blood tests on him and arrange transfusion. He was required to pay 1200 Naira for the tests. That's less than $10. He didn't have it. I had to part with some of the meagre funds I had with me. For me, although I was already on the National Health Insurance Scheme, which the Obasanjo administration implemented for all Federal Government workers, I couldn't access NHIS for my treatment at that hospital because my NHIS coverage is domiciled to a particular hospital.

In all these things, I can prove to you that if anyone should be agitated about the level of infrastructural decay and inadequate social services in Nigeria, I should be one. Yet my understanding of the whole picture is that the infrastructural decadence prevalent in the country is a direct result of lack of fiscal order and sanity.

My own 7-point agenda

Seriously, I wish I were in government and could get to draw up plans and projects. If I have the opportunity to draw up a good-governance plan for the country at this time, it will go as follows:

Point 1:   June 2011 – Release $1.5 billion to the Police force to create a national police link that links up all police station in the country and have a dedicated emergency call number that's not more than 3 digits and easily memorable. Specify December 2011 as completion date. Make the Inspector General of Police and Minister of Police Affairs responsible for this agendum. Order 109 helicopters for the Police aerial patrol. If by December 2011, the National Police link is not in place, the IG and Minister should be ready to face prosecution. I tell you it is doable. The Nigeria Police seem to be reliant on physical barrier methods for crime prevention. It is archaic and sordid. The Police Link will be a first step to transform the fight against crime from physical to intellectual. It will help the police to collect, collate and analyse information. That is modern crime fighting.

Release $500 million to the prison services and the judiciary. Request that records of all inmates and workers in all Nigerian correctional facilities should be networked into a secure electronic network. The Attorney General of the Federation should from his desk, in his office be able to say, for instance, *"there are 51,213 inmates in Nigerian prisons as at today. 6 of them have been awaiting trial since 1994 over stolen tubers of yam. Why?"* When things like these are done to strengthen the image and effectiveness of the legal system, the populace would trust the system more and would be willing to share information with the crime fighting organisations.

Court records too should be electronically archived and linked. Presently a man could walk in into a court and get a sworn declaration of age that he is 32 years old, and could return to the same court within a few months and also get a sworn declaration that he is 28 years old and the court would have no means of easily reconciling the records and detecting the fraud. It doesn't cost so much to make the system more fool-proof. Does it?

Fixing the police, prison and judicial services should be first agenda and there should be designated officers who would have the responsibilities of updating this information. I know Nigerian agencies are not good at keeping information up to date. As at this morning, I still checked the website of the presidency. The name of President Goodluck Jonathan still has the appendage GCON, whereas the gentleman has been decorated GCFR for nearly a year now. I wonder who is responsible for updating the website. When I think of the police link, the model I am thinking about is not like that of the website of the presidency that would not be updated for months upon months. I am thinking of something real-time, like transaction posting in banks.

Point 2: July 2011 – Release $1 billion to the Federal Internal Revenue Service. Give them a timeline of December 2012. At the end of December 2012, every taxable person in Nigeria should have a unique taxpayer identification number. Ideally A person should be able to walk in to the FIRS and see a record of the total amount of taxes he has ever paid in his lifetime.

Mandate the FIRS to liaise with the US IRS and understudy how the IRS uses taxpayer identification numbers to track and curb corruption.

Request the FIRS to come up with a progressive income tax schedule. Notify financial institutions that taxpayer identification numbers will be required for banking from January 2013.

Release funds to the Vehicle Licensing agency and lands and housing ministries to overhaul the system of vehicle licensing and certificates of occupancies for properties. Vehicle licences should be granted only upon presentation of a valid taxpayer identification number. Do the same for certificates of occupancy for houses.

Point 3: August 2011 – Release $1 billion to the Federal Ministry of works for the construction of toll plazas across the Federal highways in the country. Actually, these would be different from what we had previously. Unlike the ones we had in the past, these new plazas should be set up as Road Maintenance Companies. They would all be separately privatised in 2012. We actually need just about 100 of such. This means each toll plaza would get $10 million, which is 1.5 billion Naira. Don't raise your eye brows yet. 1.5 billion is not too much for a toll plaza company. The actual toll gate building and its facilities would be built at about 500 million Naira. Then each toll plaza would have road reconstruction equipments of its own worth about another 500 million Naira.

You see, Nigeria measures about 900,000 square kilometres. If you break that into squares of 100 kilometre, you would get just about 90 such squares that measure 100 kilometre on all sides. My idea is that we should build toll plazas for road maintenance companies strategically placed on our expressways. Each company would be responsible for maintaining all federal roads within its 100 kilometres radius. If you place one such at Ore for instance, the company would be saddled with maintaining all roads within 100 kilometres radius from Ore. It will maintain 100 kilometres towards Sagamu, 100 kilometres towards Benin, 100 kilometres towards Akure, 100 kilometres towards Igbokoda, etc. The toll plaza would collect the tolls from vehicles approaching it from these routes. The tolls would be collected electronically using a system of touch smartcards. So no cash will actually be handled at the plazas. When you set up each plaza, 500 million Naira will go into building the plaza, 500 million Naira will go into road maintenance equipment for the plaza, and 500 million Naira will go into take-off road repair materials for the most critical repairs that need to be immediately done on these expressways.

The problem with our roads is not that the government is folding hands doing nothing as most of you would say. The problem is that the method of maintenance is wrong. Most repairs are done on a contract basis. There are all sorts of holes on Nigerian roads. There are the pot holes (those small holes that look like bowls), and the bath holes (where your vehicle would have to take a complete dip in the mud, right in the middle of the expressway). The problem is that most times, the government has to wait for a road to fall into serious disrepair before it can award a contract for its repairs. If the damages on a particular road are not extensive enough to justify the process of a significant contract award, then the road doesn't get fixed. It shouldn't be so. The road maintenance should be a permanent contract awarded to each toll plaza company. Yeah, I know there is the FERMA – Federal Road Maintenance

115

Agency. But I have once heard a FERMA official saying that if his agency needed to patch a single pot hole, it doesn't have the money at its immediate disposal. It has to write memo to Abuja and request for funds to patch that small hole and the process could take nearly a month. Most times, then, FERMA has to wait until there are sufficient holes and bad portions on a road to justify the *wahala* of sending memo up and down. That's awkward. You know how many holes there are on Nigerian roads? It is not practicable to write a memo for every hole and wait 4 weeks for the memo to complete its cycle. It means in effect that the reasons we have many bad roads is because the roads were "not bad enough" to justify the process of repairing them early enough and prevent them from getting worse. Common, things can be done more systematically.

Point 4: September 2011 – release $1 billion for the establishment of a National Transport Company. What's the use of this? It's a first step towards deregulating the downstream oil sector. Nigeria spends averagely $4 billion yearly subsidising imported refined petroleum products. The government's headache over the years has been how to remove this subsidy and use the funds for other developmental plans. It has never worked. Of course, it won't ever work because the approach has always been wrong.

See, I have had a tooth extraction thrice. Before any dentist would pull out your tooth, she would inject a local anaesthesia into your gums. You won't feel the pain when the tooth is being removed. But the various Nigerian governments over the years have always tried to extract the fuel subsidy without injecting a prior "local anaesthesia" into the economy. First inject $1 billion into the transport sector, import 5,000 luxurious buses (coaches) into the country. Build a nationwide interstate transport system, make it cheap and efficient. I can assure you that at a petrol pump price of 120 Naira per litre as against the present 65 Naira per litre, an efficient national road transport system will provide interstate journeys to Nigerians at lesser prices than we presently pay for it. You want to try it? Put 200 luxurious buses between Lagos an Ibadan let the buses run on schedule every 10 minutes. Put the price at 300 Naira per seat. Earmark fuelling costs at 110 Naira per litre (you would actually buy fuel at 65 Naira per litre and keep the difference of 55 Naira per litre in an escrow account) to see how you would balance out if you were actually paying 110 Naira per litre. You would find that the business would still run profitably at a fuel cost of 110 Naira per litre, with air-conditioned buses at 300 Naira per seat. But what do we presently get? We pay 700 Naira per seat between Ibadan and Lagos at a fuel cost of 65 Naira per litre and in rickety buses. The Government should take over inter-state transportation for a start but not for too long. It should be done in a 24-month 3-phase plan and fully privatised.

The goal is to create 3 independent national transport companies and privatise them all within 24 months. Start, say the Freedom Line, today with 5,000 buses. Let it run a nationwide low-cost interstate transportation network and as soon as you have done that, withdraw a third of the petroleum subsidy. It means, fuel price per litre might go to 80 Naira per litre but people won't mind because you have already provided them an efficient and cheap public transport system. Sell off the company – fully privatised after 8 months, and start another one, say Peace Line, with another set of 5,000 buses. The Peace Line would compete with the Freedom Line and it too would be sold off after another 8 months. When you launch the Peace Line, you cut off another third of the petroleum subsidy but fares for the Freedom Line and Peace Line would remain low because the fares were fixed at an assumption of an unsubsidized fuel – say 110 Naira per litre. Trust Nigerians, we would complain, but the majority of the complaints would come from car owners who prefer to travel in their own cars – for egoistic reasons. The majority of the people would be pleased though, and in a process of time even the car-owners would find it more reasonable to travel in the cheaper air-conditioned luxurious buses if it is well-organised and well-maintained. By the 16th month, you are lunching the 3rd line, Unity Line, and that also would be sold off in another 8 months. Thus, over a 24-month period, you would have introduced Freedom, Peace and Unity lines, each with 5,000 luxurious buses and efficient nationwide operations competing against each other. More importantly, you would have freed the nation from the fuel subsidy monster that drinks 600 billion Naira annually.

I know Nigerians don't want to hear anything that has to do with increase in pump prices. There is no argument you make to the Nigerian public that would convince us that fuel subsidy is bad for our macroeconomics. We don't want to pay more for fuel and transportation. But in fact we do pay more through the subsidies than we would be paying if there were no subsidies. I think that's entirely another argument that I would have to deal with in a separate book – however, that's a very important point on my own 7-point agenda.

We need large national transportation companies – that would run efficiently and eliminate the present "garage-boys"-controlled transportation system. You may not realise it, but we actually pay to keep the hemp-smokers and touts at those bus stops because it is from what we pay – rather, from what's exorbitantly extorted from us – that they get their "cuts" to smoke cannabis. And look at it, you get to the bus stops, and you'd find 6 buses all trying to pick up passengers for the same destination at the same time. The system is very inefficient. If the federal government puts in $3 billion dollars over a 24- month period to create 3 separate national companies that would run interstate transportation, it would help the government to douse the tensions of pulling off the $4 billion wasted in "bad-tooth" petroleum subsidies annually. You can't have put in a 15-000-luxurious-bus system in place and not win the argument about withdrawing the fuel subsidy.

Point 5: October 2011 – Launch a massive Social Security and Adult Literacy Administration. One of the major problems hindering development plans in Nigeria is Adult Literacy. Several plans a government might want to carry out becomes impossible when the government cannot effectively communicate with the people. You would have to deal with the problem of adult illiteracy in this country if you must move the country forward.

In 2004, I was visiting a relative in Abuja and went with him to his office – the Federal Ministry of Finance. Could you believe that a young man, probably about 35 years old, came into the office complex with his wares but couldn't speak any other language besides the Hausa language! He had a bag with him containing clothes. He couldn't speak English and couldn't speak even pidgin. My host and I are Yoruba and couldn't understand or speak Hausa. We had to get a Hausa guy from the next room to interpret. You know what? Even the value of money had to be called out to him in his dialect. It was sickening. How do you even get to explain to such a man that it was not proper for him to hawk his goods in a Federal Ministry building when you can't communicate with him? Whatever that means to you, my business in the matter is that the guy obviously makes some income whether he can speak the country's official language or not, and I would need him to pay taxes if I were the president, and I must therefore solve the problem of communicating with him. The Federal Government must develop a plan to eradicate adult illiteracy within the next 10 years. And it should be launched without further delay.

One of the functions of the Social Security Administration would be to provide social services and succour to the destitute, the aged and the unemployed.

For the unemployed especially, I think it is absolutely demoralising for young people to have gone through 18 straight years of formal education only to face the prospects of remaining unemployed for as long as only God could tell, and with no support whatsoever from the society. Senators and House of Representative Members get severance packages worth millions of Naira. Can we afford to give graduates who participate in the National Youth Service Scheme some decent severance packages too? If you share what each Senator gets as a severance package to 1000 NYSC members, they would be more than glad.

Point 6: November 2011 Raise electricity tariff to commercial levels and speed up the plan to deregulate the power sector. People don't want to talk about this. The argument is that anything that will compound the suffering of the people by raising costs should be avoided. The truth, however, is that all these subsidised systems does no one any good. See, I pay averagely 1000 Naira per month for PHCN electricity for my 3-bedroom flat. But total hours supplied from PHCN is often less than 12 hours averagely for the day, at the best times. In addition to what I pay PHCN, I spend averagely 500 Naira per day buying petrol for the generator. If PHCN would rather give me 24-hours per day non-stop supply for 9000 Naira a month, which would be at a tariff 4 times their present rates, I would prefer that. It would make more sense than paying 1000 Naira to PHCN and then having to spend an additional 15000 Naira on fuelling the generator for the month. If the PHCN raises tariffs to commercial levels such that the sector can be rapidly privatised to provide a round-the-clock steady supply, I can choose how to manage my electricity consumption and cut my consumption to my income. But at least the assurance and comfort that the electricity is always available will be there. The tariff should be raised to commercial prices in order to encourage private investors to come in into that industry. In the process of time, competition would bring in price adjustments and at the same time, Nigerians would become better at managing power consumption. Some people would leave on their air conditioners and travel out of state for several weeks. The air conditioners would go on and off as PHCN cuts and restores power. If these people pay commercial rates for power consumption it would possibly encourage them to use power more reasonably.

The rate of development of the country will always be determined by power supply. But we cannot have an efficient power supply system if we don't deregulate that sector. There is no need to be sentimental about it – the only way to speed up the deregulation is to make that industry commercially viable for any interested investor. And the only way to make that possible is to let the tariffs be fixed at commercial rates. It will hurt at the beginning, but never for too long.

Also in November 2011: Present a $60 billion tax-financed budget for 2013 to the National assembly. What! You may not like me for that, but the nation has to make a quantum leap from being the self-deluding oil-can-never-run-dry economy to a tax-paying economy and the time is NOW!

Actually, I would like to start with two unpopular taxes – property tax and wealth tax. It's not a big deal, but I want to take 0.1% of the value of your real estate every year and put it in the government purse. And I want to take also 0.5% per year of your total net worth above 10 million Naira. The only problem is that I want to harvest retrospectively with effect from May 29, 1999. It means that for a start, I would collect 1.2% of the value of your real estate and then 6% of your total worth above 10 million Naira; thereafter you would pay 0.1% and 0.5 % for the taxes respectively.

See, most of you are self-centred. If I say I want to collect 1.2% of the value of Obasanjo's real estate, or Babangida's real estate, or Dangote's real estate, and take 6% of their total net worth above 10 million Naira, you would say that's too small. If I say the same of your property and net worth, you would say "why?" You want to keep spending oil money. Is it your money? *Oil well dey your papa village?* Keep spending it! I don't mind. It will soon dry up, though, and I wonder what would become of Nigeria then.

I look at Lagos and it looks to me that Lagos alone has real estate value in the region of $1 trillion. You think that's exaggerated? Go out and assess the property value of Ikoyi alone, not counting Magodo, Lekki, Ikeja, Victoria

Island. Why should such a vast wealth not be commercialised? I look at Abuja and see Maitama, Wuse, and Asokoro . . . such a vast wealth. There are many houses worth 500 million Naira in these neighbourhoods. All I want to do is collect 0.1 % of that value annually and put it into the government coffers, but you will have to pay cumulatively for the past 12 years in the first instance. So, people living in 950 Million Naira mansions in Ikoyi should put 11.4 million Naira into the government purse for a start and put in another 0.95 million Naira annually.

How about people who have big houses, but no cash? Exactly, that's where I am going. Let them mortgage and bring the taxes. The mortgage market in Nigeria is practically non-existent. We have to stimulate it by any means possible and one way to stimulate it is to introduce property tax such that people who have valuable property but no cash can mortgage their houses and use part of the funds to pay the property tax and part of the funds to do business.

Dangote is on Forbes list? Very good. I learnt that other Nigerians are there too. I'm told they are worth $15 billion between them. Good news. I mean, good tax news. All I want to do is put 6% of that into the government purse and put 0.5% more annually. (Common, what's 6%? You see all those countries that you wish Nigeria could be as developed as, the rich people out there pay as much as 40% tax).

Of course, there are so many other Nigerians that are not billionaires but if you combine their net worth above 10 Million Naira, you will get probably some $2 to $4 trillion. I want to take 6 % of that for a start and take 0.5% more per annum. And you can bet, that will be more than we get from oil.

Why would I be presenting the 2013 budget to the national assembly in 2011? Of course because I know it would take a lot of debate before they would approve a switch to a tax-based economy and more because it seems the process is often so slow that it has to be started 13 months earlier.

Point 7: Keep on looking for new ways to fund the country and make things run efficiently for the rest of my tenure in office with or without oil money.

Now you see, that there hasn't really been too much money, but the problem of how to spend it remains with us.

Chapter 8

I Wish You Only The Best

"... then choose for yourselves this day whom you will serve ..."
-     Joshua 24: 15, New International Version

The Eyes of a Child.

One of the best novels I have ever read is *"Eyes of a Child"*, by Richard North Patterson. It's a great story. I actually read it with the eyes and mind of a child. If you don't mind, I like life that way. I look at everything as a child. It has helped me to learn from everything. I learn from books. I learn from movies. I learn from documentaries. I told you earlier, I had picked "cleverness, good governance and good luck" from a programme on the National Geographic channel.

When I watch a movie, not only the plot but also a few lines from the movie just manage to stick and they are ever with me. I was visiting a friend and watched with him a movie titled *The Stepford Wives* – man, that's some crazy movie. But I loved it.

One line stuck from *The Stepford Wives* – a lady was being fired. Instead of being told "you are fired", it was put nicely to her as "We wish you only the best". I laughed.

Consciously or otherwise, I have from then used those words virtually every day. When I'm dismissing someone, I wouldn't say, "Please go away", I would just say "I wish you only the best". Or, might find some variations – like "please do enjoy the rest of the month" – it means, actually, "you've so much upset me, and I wouldn't want to come across you for the rest of the month". Crazy, isn't it. But it's a nicer way of passing it across. However, there are times I'm less sarcastic and I actually do wish people only the best and nothing but the best.

One of my "sons" would always believe that anytime I wish someone only the best, it means "good bye". As I was writing this book, I took a day out to process the renewal of my visa. When I told my "son" that the final chapter of the book would be titled "I wish you only the best", his eyes suddenly widened. "I hope", he said to me, "that Uncle T is not saying a final good bye to Nigeria, this one that you are wishing Nigeria only the best". I laughed. I tried to re-assure him, "Oh no, I'm not. I'm committed to Project Nigeria and will do my bit to make sure it works . . . and that things work out. I won't abandon the country just yet".

But Really I Wish You Only the Best.

There are times, I don't feel "proudly Nigerian", though. Especially, when I want to type on my computer and power failure means I won't have electricity for a whole day. Or, when I encounter my compulsory friends, the police. Or when I see paper posters – "Vote for me, Change is Coming" – "Vote for me, Accountability 2011" – "Vote for Me, Electricity 2011" – "Vote for Me, I will Father You", "Vote for Me, I will Mother You". Or, when I encounter university graduates that can't speak English correctly – whereas, English is our official language. At such times, I would croon to myself "If I have a wing, I will fly; if I have a wing, I will fly; fly away, fly away; over the mountains over the seas, while my parents wave for me". Actually, that was a nursery rhyme that stuck, like a variation of it "If I have a wing like a dove". Yet I know many Nigerian youths would rather fly away.

I have had the opportunity to leave this country permanently. It would have taken me so much "work" to leave the country permanently; but I could just have done that. See, I have friends in Canada, United States and the United Kingdom whom I guided on filling the visa applications and attending visa interviews and they succeeded. There have been people whose visa applications were denied and I helped prepare appeal statements and guided on how to go about it, and they won the appeals. But the idea of giving up on Nigeria and saying "it has never worked and would never work" has not found a home in me. Every day I look forward to a glorious Nigeria, one we could be proud of everyday wherever we go.

On the cover of this book, the most prominent face is that of the incumbent president, Goodluck Jonathan, and by the title, you may have assumed that this is just one more book campaigning for the president. If you say so, I won't seriously contend. I like the guy. He's cool. I mean, if you know what "cool" means. But I am not asking you to vote for him, if you don't want to. I won't tell you to vote for Jonathan or vote for Buhari or vote for ... how many names would I list now out of the 18 candidates?

However, whoever you choose to vote for, be sure you are voting for the best. If Jonathan himself should read this book, I am sure there are many things he wouldn't like in it. If his opponents read it, there are things in here they might want to use against Jonathan's campaign. So, I don't want you to see it as a pro-Jonathan book.

... the outcome is determined by strategy, skill and a little luck'. Shine your eyes. Look for any candidate that has the entire three, then vote for that person. Never forget if anything works well, it's because there's good luck in it.

Am I pro-Jonathan? No, I'm not. Am I anti-Jonathan? No, I'm not. If you want me to speak in exact terms about Goodluck Jonathan, I would rather not speak because I should be politically neutral in public. However, if you insist and really press me hard to reveal my choice, I would tell you, "before you cast your vote, remember that 'as in any battle, the outcome is determined by strategy, skill and a little luck'. Shine your eyes. Look for any candidate that has the entire three, then vote for that person. Never forget, if anything works well, it's because there's good luck in it".

James W. Bartley Jr. has gone beyond the common status quo to explore a subject that most authors do not have sufficient experiential credentials to delve into. He practically reflects on his more than 60 years experience of walking with God to bring many into an awe-striking deeper communion with God. His book, Worship that pleases God gives an accurate insight into the inexhaustible subject of Worship – as an invaluable asset in the Man-God relationship. Being a retired Professor of theology, Dr. Bartley has successfully made a holistic and unassailable exposition of worship – as a theme that finds its root in the book of Genesis and continues to Revelation in the Bible, while his academic perception lends credence to his work. Worship that pleases God is not just a book that enriches the knowledge of inquisitive readers; Dr. Bartley has carefully sequenced it in such a manner that even the least motivated reader will simply find the wave of his discovered supernatural worship pattern so irresistible.

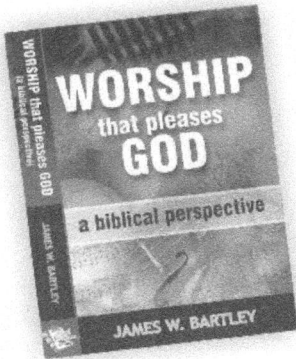

Also from Baal Hamon Publishers:

The Fatherless – a novel by Erin Inman
February 2008, 420 pages, 5.5' x 8.5'
ISBN 9780756914 (Paperback: US $17.99, UK £13.99)
Category: Fiction

Nick Pierce, a talented young boy whose singular obsession is music, finds himself overturned from a lonely life with his grandmother in Wichita, Kansas to the rather strange atmosphere of life in Western Kansas with the father he had never met. Although a friendly neighbor couple takes Nick under their wing, circumstances in life and his father's attitude work against him. In search for a way to fulfill his uttermost desires, he enters into a world of the unknown – a stranger world that leads him into questioning right from wrong. In the face of a life-threatening sickness, Nick wonders if life could offer him a little more, if music may still flow from his fingers, in praise to the Father-God.

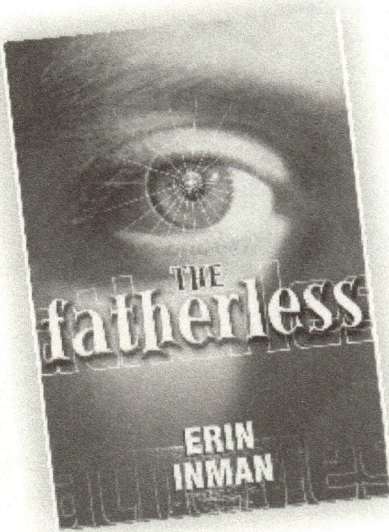

Order from www.baalhamon.com

Also from Baal Hamon Publishers:

Take Me Home Windrider – by Jeff Knighton
July 2010, 264 pages, 5.5' x 8.5'
ISBN 9784956500 (Paperback: US S15.99)
Category: Non-fiction

God uses nature to teach us His ways. God has taught Dr. Knighton to be a true Christian from his uniquely rich experience as a ranch hand in Texas. It was there that he enjoyed the tough but fulfilling labors of working with horses and cattle. The work offered plenty of hours under the deep Texan sky, in both kind and harsh weather, to examine his own spirit as he rode pasture observing nature, and tending to the cattle under his watch. This book captures the reflections that have given Dr. Knighton a perspective on life unique to those who have been privileged to spend time as a working cowboy which over the years has enhanced his work as a teacher and preacher. These reflections have been used as discussion starters in small group Bible studies, and as illustrations in preaching. They afford the reader an adventurous ride in the inner man with Christ.

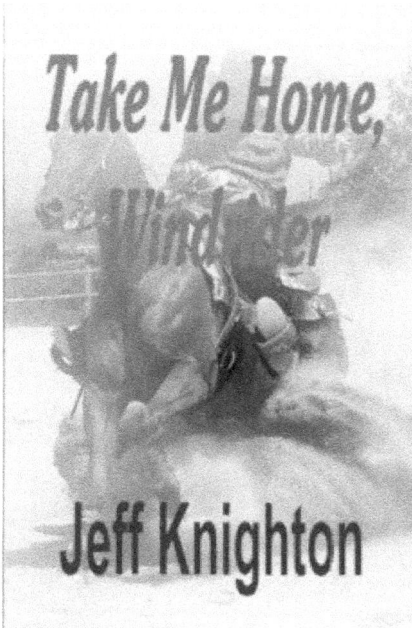

Order from www.baalhamon.com

Also from Baal Hamon Publishers:

Does God Truly Exist? – by Temitope Oyetomi
August 2006, 360 pages, 6' x 9'
ISBN 9780756825 (Paperback: US $17.99)
Category: Non-fiction

Archbishop Akinola, Primate of the Church of Nigeria (Anglican Communion) 2000 – 2010, commends this book as a "valuable material for anyone tired of dodging the questions". Indeed, it is one book that has "raised a fathom of questions" as yet another Bishop - a PhD-holder - observes in the foreword. However, the tact with which the author resolves many of these questions is scholarly and engaging. The author writes with confidence and his arguments are intelligent and highly persuasive: facts and their interpretations are presented in a style that is approachable, digestible and amenable to reading by a wide audience. Ordinarily, one might think of it as a book for those who are in doubt of God's existence. Of course, it is. But it will be more applicable to those who are sure that God exists and who believe they are worshiping the true and living God. "Who really is the true and living God" and "how best can one relate with God" are the ultimate quests of the book. Drawing answers from science, religion and philosophy, the author has contrived a rare blend "that will plausibly challenge every mind". No wonder a Baptist minister recommends it "to all people no matter their religious persuasions". It is certainly an intellectual masterpiece.

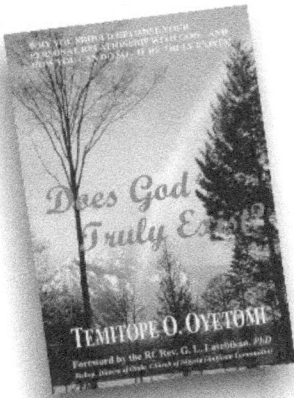

Order from www.baalhamon.com

www.ingramcontent.com/pod-product-compliance
Lightning Source LLC
Chambersburg PA
CBHW021341290326
41933CB00037B/330